T0090518

# You Are Enough:

## The Journey to Accepting Your Authentic Self

Prose and Poetry Exploring Philosophies of Self-Love, Identity, Community, Resiliency, Spirituality, Activism, Artistic Expression and more…

JACQUES FLEURY

authorHOUSE

*AuthorHouse™*
*1663 Liberty Drive*
*Bloomington, IN 47403*
*www.authorhouse.com*
*Phone: 833-262-8899*

*Published by AuthorHouse  05/30/2023*

*ISBN: 979-8-8230-0790-0 (sc)*
*ISBN: 979-8-8230-0789-4 (e)*

*Library of Congress Control Number: 2023908544*

For permission requests, write the author at:

authorjacquesfleury@gmail.com.Website:www.authorsden.com/
Jacquesfleury

*The following poems and articles have been previously published in books, anthologies and literary magazines: "Shimmer": Oddball Magazine (OM); "Taking Care of Yourself: Mind, Body and Spirit": Spare Change News (SCN), "You Are Enough: The Journey to Accepting Your Authentic Self": Spirit of Change Magazine (SOCM); "Musings on the Flowering Spring of Everyday Souls": Soul {Anthology of Poems}, (book) Edited by Sourav Sarkar, "Nothing 'Blue' About Blue Man Group": OM, "Only You Have the Last Say in Your Mental Health Plan": (SOCM), "Hope-in-Haiku": Oddball Magazine, Lessons Learned: An Ode to Mr. Powers: Tanbou Trilingual Press, MT (modified title), "A meditation on Romantic Love at Lyric Stage's 'The Last Five Years'": OM, "Sweat Posits Race, Class and Friendship at the Huntington…": OM, "Witch Casts Just the Right Spell (or Does She?)": OM, "I Hear Something You Can't Hear…": OM, " Exploring the Tension between Individuality and Conformity Amidst a Terrifying and Abusive atmosphere at a Catholic School in Haiti" (MT) : SCN/ What's Up Magazine (now defunct), "Dance the Dance Slowly: What a Dying Teen Can Teach You about Living" (MT): SCN, "The Brink of Summer's End: Celebrating the Authentic Spirit of the Seasons": SCN, "The Detriment of Pride: Learning to Let Go and Probing My Belief in a Higher Power" (MT): SCN, "In North Carolina, What I Learned During a Spiritual Retreat Sharing Space With White Supremacist" (MT): SCN, "Exploring the Identity of an Iconoclastic Pioneer: My Mother" (MT) SCN, "Exploring the Identity of an MIT Alumni and Community Visionary: Johnny Monsarraton" (MT): SCN, "TOUGH: Exploring the Contentious Issue of Masculinity in Contemporary Society" (MT) SCN, "Exploring the Arts: Resilient Women Dreaming Big in the Movie 'Dream Girls'" (MT) SCN, "Exploring the Arts: Celebrating Perpetuating and Challenging Stereotypes in the Lgbtqia Community in 'Another Gay Movie'" (MT) SCN, "Exploring the Arts: the Community Arts Center Offers an Alternative To Violence":

SCN, "Exploring the Arts: Spearheaded by Harvard University Alumni Doug Holder, the Annual Somerville Writers' Festival Celebrates Camaraderie and Creativity amongst the Literary Intelligentsia" (MT): SCN & Somerville Times, "Exploring Unity in Community at the Annual Urban Walk for Haiti": SCN & The Bridge), "Celebrating Community as the First Baptist Church Deemed Historical Landmark Celebrates 190 Years of Service to the Cambridge Neighborhood And Where Dr. Martin Luther King Jr. Once Spoke" (MT): SCN, "Haiti Also Rises: The History of Haiti's Resiliency against International Cruelty" (MT): SCN," Exploring the Buoyant Spirit of Haiti in the Beijing Olympics": SCN, "Dancing with Demons: A Mental Health Malady Survivor Story": (MT): SCN.

# Books by Jacques Fleury

*Sparks in the Dark: A Lighter Shade of Blue, A Poetic Memoir*

*It's Always Sunrise Somewhere and Other Stories*

*Chain Letter to America: The One Thing You Can Do to End Racism,*
*A Collection of Essays, Fiction and Poetry Celebrating Multiculturalism*

You Are Enough: The Journey to Accepting Your Authentic Self

## Anthologies as Contributing Author

*Cooch Behar Anthology: Ed. Sarkar, Sourav*
*Soul {Anthology of Poems}: Ed. Sarkar, Sourav*
*God Anthology: Ed. Sarkar, Sourav*
*Time Anthology: Ed. Sarkar, Sourav*
*Poets of the Year 2022: Ed. Sarkar, Sourav*
*Litterateur Redefining World January 2023: Ed. Anthru, Shajil*
*Class Lives: Stories From Across Our Economic*
*Divide: Ed. Collins, Chuck et al.*
*Eden Waters Press HOME Anthology: Ed. Brudevold, Anne*

To my inner child: you can finally say now
what you could not say then...

# Contents

## Part III: The Arts

## Part IV: Community

## Part V: Resiliency

## Part VI: Advocacy

## Part VII: Activism

## Part VIII: Acceptance

"La joie se porte, le bonheur se cultive" or
"Joy is worn, happiness is cultivated."
**--French Proverb**

# *Prologue*

Why should you read this book when there are many other books with similar titles and subject matter in the saturated literary market place? Well first, I offer a multidimensional, multicultural, multilingual perspective. I put forth a Francophone and Haitian-American frame of mind being that I am a trilingual speaker of French, Haitian Creole and American English. These cultural influences fused together to bring intriguing elements of reasoned judgments and multiple ways of understanding and expressing ideology. Second, the literature in this book is not your typical dusty purely academic dissertation on soul searching and self-reckoning. It is a manifestation of soul authenticity in action. It is a purposeful yet at times playful amalgamation of neurodivergent poetry, stories, essays, book and theater reviews, and interviews with community leaders and literary figures from Massachusetts Institute of Technology (MIT) and Harvard University. All with a connecting theme of personal authenticity: that is being true to one's self in all aspects of one's life. It encompasses spirituality, identify, artistic expression, community, resiliency, advocacy, activism and activism and ultimately acceptance of life as is rather than as you wish it to be. Because "The resistance to the unpleasant situation is the root of suffering... Love doesn't choose; psychology doesn't have a campaign slogan or subcategory for suffering. Healing is independent of political choice..." as eloquently said by spiritual guru Ram Dass.

Why did I write yet another book? This is my fourth time stepping up to the author's podium. I thought I had said everything I needed to say in my last book. The truth is, I did not intend to write another book. My last book released in 2019, just before the Covid19 pandemic hit. Twenty twenty sequestered us all for our own "safety" from each other while the Corona Virus was in an upward trajectory with person-to-person infections incubating and multiplying at accelerated rates. Hence, I, like the rest of the world, had ample time to reflect. I no longer could use the excuse "I'm too busy" for this or that. I forced myself to face my hitherto business and meet head-on with the man in the mirror staring back at me and ostensibly saying "now what? This was the time, if I was unknowingly running from myself—to stand in front of that bleak mirror and face whatever it was I was running from. The path to awakening can be winding and at times unyielding. Perhaps I was avoiding dealing with certain family members, or certain so-called "friends" or even avoided conceivably uncomfortable social interactions or what have you. Nevertheless, whatever it was I could have possibly been running from, I could not do so anymore due to our collective pandemic impasse. Therefore, I started writing to explore my inner thoughts and feelings. Moreover, as soon as things started to open back up, I started venturing out to the libraries to do research and see LIVE Theater to write play reviews and started writing about my burgeoning spirituality and poetry to submit to anthologies and online publications. The result is the book you are holding in your hands right now. Most of the writings are pandemic era musings and explorations of my inner and outer worldviews. Some are both published and unpublished gems I discovered in my literary repertoire over the years. We are now in 2023 and looking back, I realize that a lot has happened since 2020. You had the contentious election of former President Donald Trump, the Covid19 pandemic, wide scale social justice protest after the killing of George Floyd, the contentions election of Joe Biden and January 6th, 2021 riots on Capitol Hill just to name a few. The writings in this book explore all of this or none of this depending on how you decide to read the book and what is relevant or irrelevant to your life experiences. Either way, you will get to explore the workings of my inner world in response to my outer environment. I grew up feeling that I could not speak up as the first-born male in my family. Partly raised in Haiti during early childhood before I came to the states as a student and praised for remaining silent about the affronts that were happening either to me or around me. I have since learned that most young black men in America remaining silent is also part of their mantra and to not show emotion in order to get or maintain their "masculine" card. For the most part, society teaches men to mask their emotions with drugs, sex and alcohol, which often result in the abuse of woman and children or beating other men to a pulp to exert their masculinity. Thankfully,

I, along with plenty of other men-- particularly black men, have since learned that it is not a sign of weakness to show emotion; in fact, it is a sign of strength to be vulnerable. Pretending that you do not have feelings about people, places and things in your life is a fallacy to the attainment of hyper-masculine ideals. Most strong masculine heroes portrayed in the movies have some type of weakness that humanizes them. Take the story of Achilles for example. In Greek mythology, the story goes that his mother, Thetis, rendered him invulnerable by plunging him in the River Styx while he was still a baby. The tricky part was that she grasped him by the heels, which were consequentially not soaked in the water; this remained, for the most part, a vulnerable part of his body; thus the birth of the colloquial term "Achilles Heel" as we know it today. Hence, the moral of the story, no matter how strong you present yourself as, you have vulnerabilities and it takes a "strong man" to admit that. In the following pages, you will find many points where I have displayed my vulnerabilities or exposed the vulnerabilities of others or society at large but at the core of it all, I wrote these essays, stories and poems to celebrate self-love and self- acceptance in spite of our own tendencies towards self-sabotaging and self-hating practices. It begs the question: are we just an amalgamation of pain and suffering that needs healing? Are we just a representation of social injustices in dire need of reckoning? Alternatively, are we just human beings seeking the perpetual progression of our consciousness in hopes of reaching a more profound understanding of our fellow human family and consequentially ourselves while mutually sharing planet Earth? This book is a reconciling recognition and implementation of the inexorable fact that no matter who you are, no matter what your differing opinions are, they are valid. You are important, you are valued, you are seen, you are heard, your voice is sacrosanct and is worthy of being listened to because you *matter* and YOU ARE ENOUGH! Don't allow those, in discontentment with their own lives, cast aspersions on your own. Keep your head where your feet are. Stop searching for the faults so that you can find the fun; bask in the merriment of the moment.

The literature is sometimes academic and at other times esoteric. It is also relatable to the human condition, all in an attempt to explore man's inner struggle against the backdrop of Global troubles. The book is a gift to my inner child and hopefully *YOUR* inner child as well, who could not speak up then but can speak up now. Our inner child who no longer have to endure being wounded and wordless, whether vicariously or directly, this book is my love letter to our collective inner child in the attainment of the ultimate love, the divine love of self! In times of distress and self-effacement, behold and remember this French proverb: "La joie se porte, le bonheur se cultive" or "Joy is worn, happiness is cultivated."

-Jacques Fleury, 2023

# *Acknowledgements*

During the longevity of my "protracted" years on this earth, it has occurred to me that when you receive an award for reaching a milestone moment in your life, even though it is visibly just your name on the plaque, the reality is it is also everyone who helped and supported you on your path. The team that saw you struggle through hardships, challenges and roadblocks to ultimately arrive at your "dream" destination, manifesting, and reaching the pinnacle of success in life.

Moreover, with that said, I would first and foremost like to thank my mother, who believed in me and was in full support of my literary aspirations from the onset and for being the fierce yet compassionate matriarch who keeps the family functioning and together. My father, the consummate businessman, retail store owner and clothes designer, thanks for making me some fabulous suits and for funding my private catholic school education that taught me discipline and perseverance, for gifting me with a visa to go to school in America and from whom I inherited my spiritual practice of Yoga! My sister Valerie for having the courage to transcend and persist and always being her authentic self and "keeping it real" in living a purposeful life and in her younger years used to play the violin for me while I did my college homework (thanks sist!). My nieces Natavia and Nyasiah for their youthful wonderment and for adding meaning to my life through their love and playfulness by hanging out with me and spending my money (at the Big Apple Circus, the movies, boat trips, eating out at our regular spot at Alfredo's etc..,). My aunt Martine for her support in reading and giving me positive feedback and encouragement whenever I sent her my published poems or articles and for always "praying for me" (thanks aunty!) In addition, to all my friends and those whom I only had brief encounters with past and present, who are part of my journey in becoming who I am as a literary artist and as a man. As the ubiquitous Television personality Rex Trailer—who had the TV show *Boom Town* on Boston's Channel 4 for about twenty years—once said to me "Everyone that you meet become part of who you are no matter *who* they are."

I would also like to thank those outside my nuclear family. Professor Carroy U. Fergurson from the University of Massachusetts, Boston for helping to inspire my spiritual journey when I took his class, *Dimensions of Learning: The Mind, Body, Spirit Connection.* My final paper for the course was on the foundations of Reiki, which was published in the *Spare Change News* and in my third book*: Chain Letter To America: The One Thing You Can Do To End Racism. Harvard University alumni, college professor,* Somerville *Times arts editor, publisher, poet and author Doug Holder;* who I worked with during my time as writer for the Somerville Times. And for having me on his Television show *Poet to Poet, Writer to Writer* at Somerville Community Access Television (SCAT) and also for featuring me numerous times in the his column *Lyrical Somerville* and in his blog *Boston Area Small Press and Poetry Scene.* Carol Bedrosian, Publisher and Editor of Spirit of Change Magazine for curating my articles, *Poets Reading the News* for publishing my poem "*Where Am I From Originally?*", poet and author Sourav Sakar for including me in several literary anthologies as a contributing author. Editor Shajil Anthru for including me as a contributing author in *Litterateur Redefining World Anthology 2023.* The diligent and benevolent staff at Center Club of Boston for their steadfast support and granting me with *The Seth Pope Employment Award* for being a small business owner and entrepreneur. Dr. Michael Chalfin for his years of spiritual guidance. Marc Zegans for his support on social media and reviewing my poem "*Branded: Black as Means of Commodity*" published in The Somerville Times's Lyrical Somerville on Aug. 12th, 2020. In addition, for penning the abridged kindle book, *Intentional Practice & The Art of Finding Natural Audience: A Framework for Artists and Professionals* intended to help artists navigate the crowded literary and artistic market place and which I've gladly put on my "wish list" on amazon. Staples Connect Small Business Directory for featuring my Author/Tutor/Writing Coach business in the link: https://www.staples.com/stores/small-business/directory/ma/cambridge/jacques-fleury-authortutorwriting-coach.html. Howard Trachtman for his tireless activism work for the mental health recovery and rehabilitation community and for featuring my books several times on his multiple list-servers. The Medford/Somerville News for featuring me yearly in THE SOMERVILLE/MEDFORD NEWS WEEKLY FAVORITE BIRTHDAY PHOTOS OF THE WEEK! Professor Neil Calendar from *Roxbury Community College* for hosting me as an author for his college writing class. The editors at Oddball Magazine Chad Parenteau and Jason Wright for publishing my poems and hosting my theater review column *Act Three with Jacques Fleury. Spare Change News* for being the first mainstream publication to publish my very first poem out of college "Awakening" and for hosting my numerous columns over the years I worked for them. Artist Bernard Aurelien for doing the cover art for my first Boston Globe featured book, *Sparks in the Dark: A Lighter Shade of Blue, a Poetic Memoir* and for continuing to be one of my loyal social media supporters of my work. Lisa and Dave of the neo-folk musical group *Sweet Wednesday* for turning three of my poems into songs in our CD *A Lighter Shade of Blue,* with all the proceeds going to Haitian charity St. Boniface. The website PRO ESSAYS: Professional Writing Services for citing my article, Fleury, Jacques: *"Discovering Fiction: The Lost of Innocence in James Joyce's Araby and Ernest Hemingway's Indian Camp*; 10 April 2012. SCN, in their essay "An Analysis of *Araby* by James Joyce". The digital research library and teaching platform *JSTOR* for featuring excerpts from my contributing article "Living beyond Class: My Journey from Haiti to Harvard" in the Cornell University Press anthology, *Class Lives: Stories from Our Economic Divide,* Bunker Hill Community College, Northeastern University and Harvard University for hosting me in their international author literary events. Finally yet importantly, The Minuteman Library Network of Massachusetts, The Cambridge Public Library's Central Branch and The Boston Public Library's Roxbury, Central and North End branches, whose been my literary sanctuary since elementary school and where I wrote all of my books and also for including my books in their circulation catalogs.

"Deep self-love is about recognizing our innate worthiness of compassion and...granting ourselves that compassion... it's about whole hearted acceptance of who we are right now...to love ourselves deeply is to honor respect and care for ourselves regardless of how we feel what we achieve how we look or anything else that is impermanent. It is self-awareness without harsh judgement and criticism..."

**Jason Stephenson,**
**Prominent Australian Meditation Coach**
**YouTuber and Podcaster**

"Enlightened leadership is spiritual if we understand
spirituality not as some kind of religious dogma or ideology
but as the domain of awareness where we experience values
like truth, goodness, beauty, love and compassion, and also
intuition, creativity, insight and focused attention."
--Deepak Chopra

# PART I

## *Spirituality*

# *Shimmer*

It is that great bundle that titillates my yearnings;
That cagey combination of blood orange sunsets and lambent moons;
Pellucid mornings and dazzling noons;
Ready made peace that would
Piece together my amorphous path,
Emblematic of my mind:
The zenith of my existence!
Harkening back to crisp wastelands of my youth;
Yearning for what was then
The great mystery of years *yet* to be golden,
Plenty of time to furnish fantasies forbidden;
Only then it dawns on me
My wish is being manifested as a
Prima facie case of disillusionment
As time lapses like a *creep!* from
Seconds–minutes–hours–days–weeks–months
And crescending years….
Juvenility transmutes to opaque memories to remember
Sitting by a river watching the water flicker;
I try with my lacquered eyes to soak in its luminosity;
Heeding echoes of forsaken adolescence like the jocular exuberance
Of tykes doing a rough-hewn dance;
Rather than be bereaved in a coffin of longing and regret
I am gradually grateful *for* LIVING!
As the precarious impermanence of life persists
Just breathe and don't resist…
Heed the following:
Resistance to existence is the root of suffering!
Nurture and trust your light and don't judge the universe,
For it is unfolding as it most likely should…
Don't be an "I am this…" or an "I am that…"
Just **BE** and like the light of forever.
You will assuredly ***shimmer!***

# Taking Care of Yourself: Mind, Body and Spirit

The matrix of human relationships has gotten exponentially more complex amidst a convoluted web of so-called social media and technological "advances" which in turn has served as potential hindrances to some human relationships in the form of highly mechanized webs of personal misconnections. Amidst the technological chaos, what's even more at risk is our innate relationship with ourselves. We are continuously losing our core inner selves to outer distractions. The evidence is palpable. Just look around, you're bound to observe groups of friends scanning their phones while sitting or walking with each other in public. People tend to quickly stare down into their phones rather than risk making eye contact with another person on the streets. Families would rather text one another endlessly rather than make a more personalized phone call. In contemporary society, we are increasingly forgetting how to engage ourselves and each other without the vexing intrusion of technology. Don't get me wrong, I am aware of the many benefits of technological progress; the real issue is to what extent do we allow ourselves to be embedded in its web before we lose our potential for instinctive connections with ourselves and each other? In this article, I just want to emphasize some key strategies about how you can be more methodical and realistic about self-care goals; thus minimizing the possibility of failure and ensuring a grader degree of success.

*Taking Care of Your Body*

An omnipresent New Year resolution is: losing weight. Most of you probably have this at the top of your list. I know I do. For those of us who are overweight, reaching this goal may mean more than mere words can express. I mean, who wouldn't like to get rid of those love handles that we find not so "lovable" anymore because they are waging a war against our waist lines and yes to some extent, our love lives as well. Our weight can be perceived as the factor getting in the way of us feeling good about our bodies and more importantly about ourselves as individuals. Our fat can be perceived as eroding our self confidence and staining our auras. So what are we doing wrong when it comes to achieving this seemingly realistic goal to lose weight? The answer is that we are often not realistic about the way we go about reaching this goal. "A resolution is a false promise we make to ourselves once a year to make ourselves feel less guilty about how we've managed our health... finances...relationships and so forth," declares Dr. Sanford Siegal, D.O., M.D., best known for the internationally popular *Dr. Siegal's Cookie Diet Weight Loss System*. He goes on to point out three reasons why weight loss resolutions fail: "1) their goals are [often] unattainable (any diet that claims that you can lose more than twelve pounds per month should be avoided); 2) they are simply too hungry to stick to their diet and; 3) the diet they've chosen produces such slow weight loss that they lose their motivation."

"Rather than harnessing yourself with a laundry list of bad habits, choose just one [goal] that you truly want to achieve in this lifetime and focus all of your attention on the one [goal]," according to Kim Simpson in an article entitled: "69 Do's and Don'ts for Successful New Year Resolutions." We often have a goal without a plan as to how we are going to pragmatically achieve this goal. My suggestion is this: first decide how much weight you want to lose and how much allotted time you hope to reach it by. Then decide what you are willing to do during that time to make your goal accessible. For example, for me, I know that I have set a goal for myself to lose 10 pounds in one month. I have set a plan to work out at least three times a week, replace breakfast and lunch with a meal replacement drink and a sensible dinner no later than 7 p.m. in the evening. Typically, you should eat three hours before you have to go to bed. I've also decided to go for a walk after dinner to burn calories and tire myself so that I can get a good night's sleep and have my metabolism high enough to melt calories off my blossoming derriere while I sleep. In addition, after reading the book *You Can Feel Good All the Time* by Dr. Robert D. Willix Jr., I learned that taking the supplement chromium picolinate can help regulate blood sugar levels, lower cholesterol, and lose weight. Although according to research the evidence is inconclusive, some reports specify that 600 to 1,000 mcg a day of chromium picolinate may help decrease hunger, curb cravings and binge eating in some people. If you do not already know, you may be wondering, *what is chromium percolate?*

According to the website Ultimate Nutrition, chromium percolate is "a mineral absorbed in foods, which helps break down fats and carbohydrates. For this reason, chromium intake is an excellent way to reduce body fat. Many food groups contain the mineral naturally, but often in trace amounts." They go on to mention food groups that contain chromium can include:

- Meats
- Grain products
- Nuts
- Spices
- Fruits and vegetables
- Beer and wine

Dr. Willix emphasized in his book that if weight loss if your primary goal, if you take one mineral supplement, make it chromium percolate. Sign me up!

Here are three of the Do's and three of the Don'ts from Simpson's list in helping you keep your weight loss goals: I resolve to…1) make just one life altering resolution, not 10 major ones. 2) I resolve to…develop a plan that includes short and long term goals. 3) I resolve to…do it daily-one goal one day at a time for one year. And now three of the Don'ts. 1) I resolve not to…procrastinate (get going now, today!) 2) I resolve not to…get overwhelmed, or discouraged by setbacks. 3) I resolve not to…grow weary, bored or burned out. But exercise and diet are simply not enough.

Most of us who are overweight start out by hating our bodies but yet expect it to corporate with us when we try to lose weight. Well I have news for you. It doesn't work that way. Your body is keenly aware of your disgust and utter hatred for it. You won't be able to trick it into thinking that you love it when you really don't. Basically, you have no other choice but to make friends with your thunder thighs and love handles if you expect it to cooperate with your weight loss regimen. You must learn to love what you've got to start with before you can expect it to work cohesively with you on any level. I know that this may sound silly but try walking around naked in your home, hopefully when no one else is there if that makes you more comfortable. By doing this, you are learning to be comfortable naked. I know it will be difficult at first because I've done it and it took me a long time before I began to get comfortable with myself. I believe by walking around naked, you are communicating to your body that you are not ashamed of it, that you love it just as it is right now. Soon, you will be able to be naked around your romantic partner without having to hide under the covers or turning off the light during sexual intimacy.

The other "love ritual" I suggest that you do for your body is stand nude in front of a mirror and allow your eyes to explore every inch of your body. At first you will be tempted to look away and find fault in every crevice of your body, however, you must try to resist that urge and over time, you will become increasingly more comfortable with yourself. Fundamentally, my point is this: if you are unable to bestow upon yourself love and respect, how can you then expect someone else to give you something that you are either unwilling or unable to give to yourself? As Whitney Houston has sung many times over: "learning to love yourself is the greatest love of all." So Stand in front of a mirror and proclaim to yourself "I am fabulous and lovable, thin or fat, housed or homeless!" Don't fall prey to what the media and popular culture tell you what you should or should not look like or your value as a human being based on your socio-economic standing. Try to overcome your most ferocious critic of all time: yourself.

Taking Care of Your Mind

Earlier, I talked about New Year resolutions and how that they are sometimes unrealistic. The particular resolution I addressed was taking better care of our bodies by learning to accept our bodies in its present condition before we can aspire to make it better. I know that in America the phrase "I am trying to lose weight" is quite literally an American mantra. However, our bodies are just one of the sums of our parts. It is imperative that we also focus on the other components like our mind. In an age when we are drowning in neo-technological novelties like the smartphones, iPhones and the internet, we often find ourselves completely distracted and overwhelmed by things supposedly designed to make our lives easier. However, we often find that these supposed "must haves" tend to complicate matters, not simplify them. One of the other intrusive and persistent distractions our mind must also contend with is mind-numbing reality TV. Now I won't be a hypocrite and tell you that I have miraculously prevailed over these things and have been able to nurture my mind with more productive and intellectually interactive pursuits like reading and writing. I too struggle with the age of overabundance of technology and reality TV. I too have found myself watching way too many episodes of reality TV, so I know firsthand of which I speak, as usual. But it is not enough to acknowledge these great hinderers of mindful adventures, we must find a way to overcome our tendencies to succumb to technological fads and resort back, to some extent, the way things were before all the aforementioned technological pandemonium.

Remember back in the day when families used to talk to each other during family dinners? Also listening to the radio before the invention of Television? Or dare I say it, read a book before seeing the movie? Nowadays, because of the influx of books being translated on the big screen, it seems like some people, whom were once avid readers, have succumbed to going to the movies or just renting the DVD and this

HAS to stop! We must be "mindful" of what we are feeding our minds. It has been said that we are only using ten percent of our brain capacity. I find this particular fact utterly astounding. We as human beings apparently have more productive potential then we actually realize. We live in a country where freethinking is encouraged and nurtured. I use the word "free" here in a relative sense because as we all probably know by now, in this our America, freedom often co-exists with oppression. In America freedom often coexists with limitation. But essentially, we have less repercussions for exercising our freedom here than anywhere else in the entire world and for that I am grateful. The freedom to think freely in this country is often taken for granted. For example, I come from Haiti; a country known for its fervent opposition to free thinking; a country that often douse the sparks of critical thinking before they have time to bloom to a full pledged fire. In school, I was never thought to exercise my mind using the ideology of critical thinking. I was thought to regurgitate what was dictated to me. I was assigned lessons that commended blatant memorization of pages and pages of text to recite in front of my teacher the next day. I was never encouraged to analyze or conceptualize the ideas of the author using my own thought process. I was simply expected to accept them as the truth of which I had to build my life around. I never learned about critical thinking until I attended college here in America. As a matter of fact, critical thinking was a graduation requirement and I took to it like a thirsty man to water. This brings me back to my point regarding making more use of our minds as freethinking Americans.

There are so many ways to enrich our minds other than strictly acquiescing to technological worship; things that will promote more critical thinking through active learning instead of yielding to passive learning through the mind numbing garbage we are often fed while scrutinizing the tube. We still have the theatre, book clubs, sports clubs, activism, visiting friends, discussing current events, reading the paper, going for walks, escaping the city to explore and meditate in the wonders of nature, attending live performances of poetry, spoken word and music, talking to each other during family dinners, learning to enjoy each other's company without the use of technology or reality

TV. You must diligently try to learn to enjoy the freedom to think you have been privileged to have this in our America. Take some time to think versus having someone else do the thinking for you. Your mind will thank you for it!

Taking Care of Your Spirit

So far, I addressed the issues of taking care of our bodies and our minds. For the body, my suggestions were learning to respect and love our bodies as it is right now before we can expect it to corporate with any significant changes we'd like to make to it, particularly when it comes to losing weight. For the mind, I expressed my acute awareness about how technology is obliterating other pre-technological methods of ways to entertain and educate ourselves, like reading, writing, attending live events and, dare I say it, talking to one another. Now, I want to talk about taking care of our spirits.

Spirituality can mean many things to many people. However, one must not confuse spirituality with religion. Religion usually means belonging to a church and practicing certain religious rituals usually on a regular basis. It also means belonging to a certain religious denominations like Catholic, Muslim or Jewish. Spirituality on the other hand tends to lean more on the liberal side. An atheist or agnostic can both be "spiritual." Spirituality to me equates with doing what makes you come alive! What makes you get up in the morning. The reasons you do the things you do. Connecting to some greater energy both in and outside of yourself. For example, I love to dance. And I love, love, love to write. When I do either of these things, every fiber of my being comes alive. I often feel possessed by a gigantic force, energy fields beyond my imagination and understanding. An energy that inspires me to do what makes me come alive and hopefully motivate others to do the same by living my life as an example. But spirituality to me means more than my love of dancing and writing.

Spirituality to me means spreading the light, either by being the candle or the mirror that reflects it as was said by philosopher and writer Edith

8

Wharton. Spirituality to me means learning who you are through personal reflection, paying meticulous attention to your internal voice telling you what it needs to be healthy, spirituality is learning to love and respect yourself for who you are and not for whom you wish you were, it's learning to make friends with your imperfections and eccentricities, spirituality is not allowing someone else to define you as a human being but being confident enough to stand up for yourself and what you believe in. You may have heard of this omnipotent saying "If you don't stand for something you'll fall for anything. Spirituality is thinking outside of yourself to reach out to others in need even when you are experiencing life's atrocities yourself, it is about being observant and aware of your surroundings, being in and enjoying the moment, it's about taking risks and overcoming the fear and anxiety that keep you from enjoying life to the fullest, it's about graduating from merely thinking about doing something you've always wanted to do, to actually do it, spirituality is about living your life with no worries or regret, it's about believing that you are not alone in this world, believing in a higher power, believing in anything other than just yourself. For example, I once thought that I was alone in this world; that everything and anything fell on my shoulders and only I had the ability to make something happen. I tell you those were not the most affable years of my life, they were the most difficult. It was only when I turned my life over to the great mystery of universal life force energy that I began to live life with less and less fear, anxiety and worry about my present and future. My life as it is right now, is the most spiritual it's ever been. I am just beginning to learn to be comfortable in my own skin, loving and respecting myself just as I am while still knowing that until the time of my death, there will always be room for improvement.

I am finally doing what I've always wanted to do with my life which was to be a professional writer and educator. I am about to incorporate another aspect of my life that has been neglected which is to travel, even exploring local hidden gems and attractions is a step in the right direction. My heightened spirituality has taught me that the only way I can attract someone in my life that would give me love and respect is after I've learned to give it to myself. I've learned that in every relationship, never to give more than you are getting. I have learned that once you aspire to be as healthy as possible, mind, body and spirit; only then will you attract someone with similar traits into your life. I once quoted Oprah Winfrey on the subject of self-care, she said "Take care of yourself, and there is more of you to give." My new found spirituality has also taught me to go with the flow, as cliché as it may sound. I have always quoted the Pulitzer prize winning author Toni Morrison (Beloved, The Bluest Eye) as saying "If you surrender to the wind, you can ride it." So ride the winds of life as far and as high as you can go, your spirit with thank you for it.

"I understood at a very early age that in nature, I felt everything I should feel in church but never did. Walking in the woods, I felt in touch with the universe and with the spirit of the universe."

Alice Walker

# Exploring the Tension between Individuality and Conformity Amidst a Terrifying and Abusive atmosphere at a Catholic School in Haiti

"Forgive me Father for I have sinned. It's been one hour since my last confession." The preceding statement was my mantra for the thirteen years I spent enduring the fear, shame, guilt, secrecy, brutality and hypocrisy in "Frere Andre" (Brother Andre) an exclusive Catholic school in Haiti, where they used to beat God into us to "save" us from our "sinful" selves!

Actually it's quite an interesting story. My father was afraid for me, for my soul. He knew that as young boys reached puberty, they tended to have… (and I say this with a whisper) a sinful desire to experiment with their –err--elongating manhoods. So he enrolled me in a rigid all-boy Catholic school to keep me holy. Boy was that a mistake!

The inception of my rebellion began ironically *in* Catholic school. It was there that I learned the detriment of labels that were attributed to us like "no good", "devil's spawn" and "sinners." The Brothers and Priests never bothered to tell us that they were sinners too. I believe that it would have made things easier for us, to know that we were not alone. I eventually succumbed to this un-holy maelstrom of fear, guilt and shame, particularly in relation to sex. We were perpetually told that we would be stricken with the wrath of God for sins we had yet to commit.

We didn't even know what sin was! We endured daily castigations for simply being imperfect beings, as if that in itself was a Sin that we had to beg forgiveness for and they, being so holier than thou, did not!

Since we were told that we were no good anyways, we logically fell into a bottomless well of sexual ecstasy through experimentation, even though we knew that God was probably shaking his head and waving his disapproving finger at us.

Some of the "sins" we were committing in retrospect were quite amusing. We used to play a game called "L'inspecteur Des Pigeons" (The Pigeon Inspector.) In the early morning when our youthful loins were swinging happily in our tight little pants like a disobedient fire horse, we devised this secret ritual to satisfy our tension-induced curiosities. Basically we were appraising the size of our instrument of "sin." We decided that the boy with the biggest—err-- "pigeon" would be the inspector. And if another boy out grew him, then *he* would be the new inspector. After the inspection, the chosen one, the one with the biggest "pigeon", would then get a private re-inspection in the boys' bathroom. Meanwhile, the rest of us would look through the keyhole watching the chosen one's bushy "pigeon" gets blown down to oblivion by the "inspector", and gasp when it eventually reached a Shakespearian crescendo then deflating to a creamy ending!

Of course occasionally we would get caught. The Brother would apprehend the "sinner", have him lie across his throbbing lap and pound his taut boyish butt with his ruler. In the midst of all this, the boy would screech while the Brother growled, as hot sweat streamed down his face, which bore a reluctant grimace to mask his sick shameful satisfaction amidst all this calamity and malediction. Sometimes he abandoned the ruler and used his bare hands. I was called to the board more than once and the Brother lingered on my buttocks just a bit longer than I thought was necessary as he proceeded to spank me. I saw this happen with the other boys, particularly the younger ones. I did not understand why I felt uncomfortable after this sacrament perpetrated by those whom were meant to protect us, not get-off on us! But today, I do. After all this humiliation, the one thing he couldn't hide was his erection. I hated being the victim of this hedonistic ritual.

School was not the only place where we explored our burgeoning sexualities. I lived with my mom and her sisters in a spacious house with plenty of room to sin in. It was there that I took my sexual experimentation to a deeper level. My boy cousins and me fooled around with the young maids and each other. Particularly during black outs! In Haiti, messing with the maids is considered rites of passage; in America it would be child abuse. All the bible-thumping adults who condemned us when they caught us and preached no sex before marriage were banging before their own weddings. Sex was never talked about. My own mother told me that when she asked *her* mother where babies come from, grandma told her that they came from the mouth!

We were constantly told that we were children of the dark; devil's spawn they called us. I was called a sinner before I even knew what sin was. The guilt and shame were constantly eroding my soul. I thought that God could never love a sinner like me. When the Catholic molestation scandal broke out, it was such a relief to hear that I was not alone. I was not the only one who was touched inappropriately, like when the Brother fondled my buttocks. It was liberating to learn that the Priests who infiltrated our budding psyches with negativity by constantly reminding us that we were sinners, which then caused us to feel unworthy of God's love, were sinners themselves. I then found the courage to say to hell with the secrets and lies, to hell with the Catholic spell! I no longer feel lower than the bottom of a bottomless well! I really tried to be "The Best Little Catholic Boy in the World", but essentially I fell off the good boy wagon and right into a tumult of sexual exploits, often squirting my guilt with rabbit speed all over the face of Catholic hypocrisy.

Today I know that sex is a healthy thing. Today, I have chosen to discriminate in most sexual situations and at least attempt to make informed decisions. Today I exercise more control over my sex, over this mighty tree, rooted in sexual repression that threatens to pop the buttons on my boxers. More importantly, I have also made my peace with my past in the Catholic Church. After re-visiting the church scene, I've concluded that God is not in a building; he/she is in my heart. I have been brought back to God and have accepted him/her in my life not out of fear, but out of love.

Nowadays, because of theatrical productions like "The Vagina Monologues" and more recently "The Penis Responds", sex is being dragged from under the covers of shame and guilt, and erections are exposed for discussion and much more--just remember, with this new found sexual liberation comes responsibility. So exercise wisdom and caution when deciding who gets to play with your sanctity. And to my fellow "Catho-holics," I say slip away from the scourge of fear, shame, guilt and criticism. Free yourself from your toughest critic—yourself—and let the good times roll!

"In everyone's life, at some point our inner fire goes out. It is then burst into flame by an encounter with another human being. We should all be thankful to those who rekindle our spirit."

--Albert Scheitzer

# The Brink of Summer's End: Celebrating the Authentic Spirit of the Seasons

The noonday sun has mellowed. The laughter of children echoing in the playgrounds has dwindled. Soon, the chilly breath of winter will be upon us, fogging up car windows in the early morning and late at night. Yep, summer is practically over and for some of us, this glacial news is mighty sour. Now is a time to reflect on the last few months. Did you keep all the promises you made to yourself back to the beginning of summer? Did you take that vacation you've always wanted to take, talk to that cutie you've always wanted to talk to, read that book you've always wanted to read, see that movie you've always wanted to see? Or did the summer days pass by you as fast as a NASCAR race car, drowning you in a smog of dust, confusion and missed opportunities? Well, you're not alone. I did not get to do all that I wanted to do either, but I sure did as much as I could do and I don't think it's necessary for me to be hard on myself for the things I didn't get to do and neither should you.

Then in late August, I decided to go on a road trip with some friends. We decided to tour some of the states of New England so that we can get to know other northern neighbors, each other and ourselves along the way. Driving down the countryside almost always leaves me mesmerized. The quiet dignity of the trees; the wide majesty of the mountains; the boldness and beauty of the sunset and the docile and gleaming offering of the moon. As we drive along the highways and back roads of New England, assimilating Chinese fire drills and switching seats with one another, we talked about things that we normally wouldn't talk about in any other circumstances. We spoke of our hopes and aspirations, joys and pains, unrequited loves, past loves, present loves and pondered about future loves that we hope would save us all during our lifetime. Sometimes, we didn't even speak at all. We just drove and rode in silence or listened to the radio and the music of our hearts.

We drove up to Jeffrey New Hampshire so that we can climb Mount Monadnock, purported to be the second most climbed mountain in the world, second only to Mount Fuji in Japan. Climbing the mountain was both challenging and invigorating. I saw all types of people climb, young and old. But I don't think I saw even one other Black person climb. I suppose hiking is not "a black thing", but I was there to challenge this stereotype. I did get some malevolent (what are YOU doing here?) looks from some of the hikers as well as some benevolent (welcome!) smiles. I decided to concentrate on the smiles.

I was able to find some time to be alone in the woods, to hear the sound of the heart of nature and so that I can feel closer to the creator. Having some quiet time to think about my life to me is a great luxury. I was able to think about what I'm doing right and what I'm doing wrong. Behaviors that I need to re-evaluate and behaviors that I need to celebrate. I thought about all the people in my life who contribute to who I am and I could not help but smile. I realized then that I have a selective group of people around me who contribute greatly to who I am and who I'm becoming. I gladly let go of toxic relationships that threaten my progress and embrace new friendships that can only strengthen me. During my vacation, I also rediscovered the power of God in my life, which forced me to re-evaluate my spiritual path.

Getting away even for a short time from my day-to-day life taught me something. It taught me that I could find happiness outside of all the "stuff" I have back in my apartment or all the accolades I often get from my community for being a writer, performer and Television personality. Being away from all of that, generated in me a sudden epiphany. I realized that other than my God, I'm all that I need. I am self-sufficient. I don't really "need" someone else to make me happy. I don't "need" someone else to give me what I can give to myself: respect, love and attention. I realized that all one need in life is to be comfortable, healthy and happy. How can I expect someone else to give me what I can't or won't give to myself? I don't believe in the notorious saying "I'm looking for my other half" because I think that one should be a "whole" person first and naturally, if I know anything about karma, another "whole" person will find *you*.

We often get stuck in our lives when we practice the same behavior but expect a different outcome. Well you may be aware of the omnipresent saying: "Insanity is doing the same thing and expecting different results." Well, I have two things to say about that! First is "be the change that you want to see" and secondly "when you change the way you look at things, the things you look at begin to change." In other words, if your whish is to see the world as a friendly place then you have to try being friendly yourself. Yes, it is that simple. Because if you choose to see the world as a friendly place then you begin to look for evidence of that. However, if you choose to see the world as a hostile place, then you began to look for evidence of *that*. It's all about the way we think about things. My point is this: as the Autumn leaves change colors, you too should try changing your thought patterns by being the change that you want to see, by changing the way you look at things and I promise you the universe will change *with* you. Remember, keep your hearts open and may the spirit be with you always!

"Do not go gentle into that good night but rage, rage against the dying of the light."

Dylan Thomas

## *Dance the Dance Slowly: What a Dying Teen Can Teach Us about Living*

"Have you ever watched kids on a merry-go-round? /Or listened to the rain slapping on the ground? /Ever followed a butterfly's erratic flight? /Or gazed at the sun into the fading night? /You better slow down. /Don't dance so fast/Time is short/The music won't last." So begins the hopeful and emotional offering of an anonymous teenager dying of cancer in a New York hospital with an estimated six months to live. We have all heard the clichéd phrases "Slow down, life is short" or "Take the time to look around and smell the roses", but in this case the inherent meaning has been further enhanced by the unpredictable behavior of cancer and the non-committal allotment of time. I too have been exposed to this calamity imposed on humanity known as the "C" word.

Before re-discovering my pressing need to write as a profession, I worked as a health care professional for about ten years. Both fortunately and unfortunately, my last three years was working at the Chilton House, a hospice residence in Cambridge. I say fortunately, because it was my most meaningful learning experience and unfortunately because it was by far the hardest. For those of you who do not know what a hospice is, it is a place for the terminally ill to make their final exit with peace, dignity and even harmony. But essentially, it is also much more than that. It is also a place for both families and patients respectively to find closure, forgiveness, joy (yes, even joy) and enlightenment. There are five stages anyone who is dying or experiencing a major loss goes through according to Elisabeth Kübler-Ross, author of "On Death and Dying". The Five Stages of Grief are:

1. Denial
2. Anger
3. Bargaining
4. Depression
5. Acceptance

It is written that "Kübler-Ross originally applied these stages to any form of catastrophic personal loss (job, income, freedom). This also includes the death of a loved one, divorce, drug addiction, or infertility. Kübler-Ross also claimed these steps do not necessarily come in the order noted above, nor are all steps experienced by all patients, though she stated a person will always experience at least two." The stage that the dying teen is most likely at is the "acceptance" stage. By writing the poem, it is apparent to me that the dying teen is making peace with her condition and is "preparing" for her untimely departure. But her message of hope goes beyond the grave.

I will print her poem in its entirety at the end of this article. But before I do, I am compelled to tell you what I learned in my years as a hospice nurse. The midnight hour had just landed, perched like a crow upon the hospice house comely garden (the crow is said to be a symbol of death). One of my patients was dying. He was a white professor from Harvard University. Of all the people he knew, I was the only one there, a "black kid" as he said, holding his hands to the end. And he turned to me and said: "Listen kid. In life, status, education and money are not what matters. What matters is what was true and truly felt and how we treated one another." After which he died one hour later. Consequently, this teenager's compassionate legacy to humanity is the following poem, which makes me feel that we should be kind to each other while we still can because she is embracing us with kindness even as she anticipates taking her final breath. Just like her poem dictates, please read it not in haste, but slowly so that you may absorb its distinctive taste. Her poem is a gift meant to be opened slowly while the music is still playing and you're still capable of dancing...

Slow Dance
By anonymous teenager

"Have you ever watched kids on a merry-go-round?
Or listened to the rain slapping on
the Ground? Ever followed a butterfly's erratic flight?
Or gazed at the sun into the
fading night? You better slow down.
Don't dance so fast. Time is short.
The music won't last. Do you run through each day on the fly?
When you ask how are
you? Do You hear the reply?
When the day is done do you lie in your bed with the next
hundred chores Running through your head?
You'd better slow down don't dance so fast.
Time is short. The Music won't last. Ever told your child 'We'll do it
tomorrow?'
And in your haste, Not see his sorrow?
Ever lost touch, let a good friendship die cause you never had time to
call And say hi?
You'd better slow down. Don't dance so fast. Time is short.
The music won't last. When you run so fast to get somewhere
You miss half the fun of getting there.
When you worry and hurry through your day,
It is like an unopened gift thrown away.
Life is not a race. Do take it slower.
Hear the music
Before the song is over."

Her dying wish is for you to pass this on to as many people as possible. Please help fulfill a last request. In this case, share as many copies of this book as you possibly can!

# If...

"You can have everything in life you want, if you will just help other people get what they want."

Zig Ziglar

If you want to learn than you *need* to listen;
If you want to understand than you *need* to converse;
If you want to internalize than you *need* to contemplate;
If you want to show compassion than you *need* to take action;
If you want peace than you *need* to be peaceful;
If you want joy than you *need* to be joyful;
If you want love than you *need* to be lovable...

"Whoever fights monsters should see to it that in the process he does not become a monster. And if you gaze long enough into an abyss, the abyss will gaze back into you."

Friedrich Nietzsche

# The Detriment of Pride: Learning to Let Go and Probing My Belief in a Higher Power

I came from Haiti with nothing more than a tepid smile and a suitcase full of hope of a new beginning. In the following paragraphs, I will elaborate on my journey since I left Haiti. I will tell you about my tumultuous excursion from having a dream to living it. How pride kept me from experiencing success with people. How the illusion of ultimate control over my life caused me much pain and disappointment. How a virtuous friend helped me to recognize God in myself, how learning to let go and let God help put my life in its proper perspective, leading me to achieve peace of mind in all aspects of my life!

I grew up as part of the middle to upper middle class in Port-au-Prince, Haiti's capital city. My father was a Tailor with his own business. I lived with my mother and her sisters in a two-story house with a pool left for them by my grandparents.

My father was particularly fanatical about education. His own father failed to support his desire to become a doctor. Therefore, he felt that being a clothes maker, designer and retail storeowner was settling for less. It was for that reason that he wanted to make sure that his children get the best education money and influence can buy. I enrolled in an exclusive all boy catholic school called *Frere Andre* (Brother Andre) located adjacent to the Haitian White House. It was there that I endured physical and psychological abuse and witnessed with my own trembling eyes the hypocrisy of the Catholic Church. Essentially, after I left, I became terribly embittered about the whole idea of God.

When Haiti was finally behind me, I was skeptical about the existence of a higher power. I then started to look to humanity for ultimate love and direction. I was gravely disillusioned, to my chagrin.

Coming to America was my mother's idea. She convinced Dad to use his position as an entrepreneur who had U.S. residency and mercantile status to get me a student's visa. He agreed to the idea, only if my mom would bring me back. My mom told him that I would only be gone for the summer. We left soon after and I haven't been back since.

My dad has since passed away today. I am saddened by the fact that he never got to see me live out my dream to become an acclaimed author. But that's all behind me now. Ahead of me is a future decorated with hope and grace.

My dream has always been to be a writer since high school. I went to Boston English High where I worked on the school newspaper and was student editor of the school literary magazine. It was there that I discovered the power of the written word.

Back in the late 1980s, in the midst of the AIDS crisis and amidst fallacious allegations (a now debunked ideology) that this hideous malady originated from Haiti unfortunately caused a rift between the African-Americans and the Haitian students. Physical fights would explode at any given moment. It was then that I wrote an article in the school newspaper sharing Haitian culture. Miraculously, the tensions diminished and some of the Haitian students even thanked me for humanizing them thus mitigating the illogical hatred felt by the African-Americans toward the Haitians.

Today, after surviving economic and linguistic hardships while adjusting to living in America, graduating from college, enduring struggles with psychological instability and essentially finding God in the midst of the debris, I can finally say I am a survivor. During the apex of my writing career, I wrote for six different publications and published my first poetry book aptly titled "Sparks in the Dark" which was featured in and endorsed by The Boston Glove on its front cover. I now choose light during times of darkness and try not to stare into the abyss too long.

As far as the issue of Pride goes, I am still in the process of making peace with my ego. Before I accepted the universal life force energy and spirit in my life, my ego determined the outcome of most of my interactions. Today, I am learning to process before I speak. I have appointed the universal energy as my guidance counselor, but also as my mediator. Fortunately, on my way to maintaining healthy relationships as a result.

When I stopped believing in a higher power, I replaced him/her/them with humanity. My mother was at the top of that list. I expected perfection from her as well as from all others in my life. Since I felt so deficient, I reasoned that everyone else had to be beyond sufficient. Fortunately, when my own mother failed to meet these grandiose expectations, I started to look elsewhere for the ultimate truth.

Miraculously, I met a spiritual diva named Nneka. When I told her that I was borderline atheist, she said with a quiet confidence: "Jacques, you can't be the way you are without believing in a higher power. You will admit to having God in your heart in due time. Until then, I will wait patiently for you to open up your heart to him."

I soon gave up the notion that I was in total control of my destiny and began to ponder the possibility that there may in fact be a God. It was only when my life threatened to fall apart, that I sought God with the fervor of a thirsty man in the midst of a drought. I gave up the illusion of control and decided to let go and let God. My life then slowly began to rearrange itself in a harmonious alignment.

Today I have made my peace with the uncertainty of humanity. Today I enjoy life's sour as well as its sweeter offerings. In the words of Pulitzer Prize winning author Tony Morrison: "If you surrender to the wind, you can ride it." Life is like the wind, you can choose to ride it or resist it. I'm choosing to ride it.

"Focus on what lights a fire inside of you and use that passion to fill a white space. Don't be afraid of the challenges, the missteps, and the setbacks along the way. What matters is that you keep going."

Kendra Scott

# *In North Carolina, What I learned During a Spiritual Retreat While Sharing Space with White Supremacists*

LAKE JUNALUSKA, N.C.-As the sun descended into the belly of the smoky mountains, I could feel my tense city slicker body melting into the serene liquidity of Lake Junaluska. Tucked away from disarray, Lake Junaluska, to me, is the heart of North Carolina. An old acquaintance once said to me, "…when you live against the breast of the earth, everything feels different" and that is most definitely true about Lake Junaluska. Recently, after receiving a scholarship from both our parent United Methodist Organization, Reconciling Ministries Network (RMN)) and my own local church, Cambridge Welcoming Ministries (CWM), my mother, some of my fellow church members and I embarked on a four day road trip to find meaning in the midst of the chaos in our lives and the world. CWM is a reconciling United Methodist Church, meaning that it affirms the worth of every human being regardless of race, creed and, particularly, sexual orientation. It was because of this that the white supremacist group, the Ku Klux Klan, protested our Church.

We are living in a time when horrific acts are still being committed against the Gay Lesbian Bisexual and Transgender community (GLBT). In recent news, it was said that gay teenagers are being killed in the streets of Iraq simply for being themselves. Despite the fact that gay visibility is becoming more and more prominent in the media with shows like "Will and Grace" and "Queer Eye for the Straight Guy" and the plethora of lgbtquia characters in the popular media, our society still have a lot of work to do. It is because the gay community have been subjected to this tragedy that the gay members of our Church resolved to seek tranquility and fraternity at the "Hearts on Fire" convocation at Lake Junaluska's retreat center.

The Ku Klux Klan, who call themselves the "White Nights", traveled from Georgia to North Carolina to stage a demonstration against what they call "Queers On Fire." Even though the majority of the church members are heterosexual identified. Their argument is that since "God hates fags", they then have no business being in the church. Then the flaming question is this, where can they go to find sanctuary? I am aware of the ridiculous ideology, that if you are not white, heterosexual, rich, able-bodied, Christian, young and male, you are then perceived to be further and further away from divinity, which is a mere fallacy. Upon knowing that the KKK were coming to crash our totally fabulous party, local North Carolina newspapers like *The Mountaineer* and *Citizen Times* capitalized by aggrandizing the KKK's demonstration, thus exacerbating what turned out to be a rather meek manifestation.

Upon learning of the KKK's then impending presence, I could not help but recollect the days of random bombings, shootings and hangings, which naturally made me feel *some* anxiety. As we came closer to the retreat center, our pastor called to warn us that there were teenagers driving in pick-up trucks with white hooded attires hanging on stakes, since the law forbids wearing them, particularly in North Carolina.

The better part of the retreat however was everything else! The drive to and from the center, worship gatherings, bible studies, the entertainment and the "miracle moments" where participants were invited to share a little about their diverse experiences within the Methodist Church. I found myself moved to share my own personal religious history having grown up in the Catholic Church, and that I never knew what "church" meant until I came to Cambridge Welcoming Ministries. It is a place where worshiping God is not based on the concepts of "guilt" and "fear", but on the foundations of love and acceptance.

Within the confines of the Carolina Mountains, I started to listen to the sounds of the red exotic songbird that is my heart. I met ubiquitous yoga therapist, self-Empowerment and reiki practitioner Jesse Lee. She quoted Oprah as saying: "Take care of yourself and there's more of you to give..." Jesse made tentative plans to appear on my then TV show "Dream Weavers" at Cambridge Community Television (CCTV). Jesse also talked about the process of authenticity, to be and become who we are. It was during one of Jesse Lee's covenant groups that I learned *my* truth: "I am what I am because of my measure; I'm not what I am because of their measure."

Speaking of authenticity, the drive to and from the center most definitely brought forth my church family's "authenticity". There is nothing like spending an exorbitant amount of time with people you thought you knew to dismiss ones illusions about each other. The conversations along the road brought temporary bouts of depression and elation, confusion and clarity, resentment and essentially disillusionment regarding who we *thought* each other were. Yet in spite of it all, I think we all came closer to the truth of our actual reality: that we are all broken pearls along the road. It was then I found that empathy and forgiveness brought me closer to *my* truth.

Also on board was the United Methodists of Color for a Fully Inclusive Church founded in 2000 according to church volunteer Randy Miller. Mr. Miller stated that the goals of the UMOCFFIC are to defuse racism, deter exclusivity, particularly of people of color. He also mentioned that heterosexual identified Bishop Mel Tolbot, president of the Black Methodists for Church Renewal has offered his unwavering support; which is a mark of their success.

We went to the mountains and heard echoes of the tiny endearing voices of prayer, patience, and perseverance. We deemed our theological task to be practical, critical, constructive, and contextual. We subscribe to the doctrine of what I call "thoughtful liberalism!" Logically, because I am was part of the CWM United Methodist Congregation, I am proudly declaring myself to be a progressive theological thinker! Our mission is to make "...disciples for the transformation of the world", redefine and reclaim our authentic and fabulously colorful and multiracial identities. Since we have already begun the journey to self-discovery, we are most definitely coming closer to the ultimate truth: our own.

I was born by myself but carry the spirit and blood
of my father, mother and my ancestors. So I am…
never alone. My identity is through that line.
--Ziggy Marley

# PART II

## *Identity*

# Who Am I?

*if you peel layer*
             *upon layer*
                 *upon layer*
*maybe then and only then*
*you will find me...*
*for i am a multilayered entity...*
*a building block of heterogeneity*
*i can be fierce and unflinching*
        *apathetic and also doting*
           *docile and also volatile*
              *lovable and also irritable*
                 *compulsive and also discernible*
*I am a man*
*I am a "black" man*
*I am an American*
*I am a "black" American*
*I am a DNA test from*
*Ancestry dot com's family tree*
*And twenty-three and me*
*I am African ancestry*
*I am Afro Haitian ancestry*
*I am European ancestry*
*I am the legacy of a middle class family in Haiti*
*I am the legacy of America's social and economic disparity*
*I am the story of Horatio Alger's characters thriving over adversity*
*I am a malady*
*I am a remedy*
*i am a rainbow*
*i am a shadow*
*I am a son*
*I am a brother*
*I am an uncle*
*I am an author*

I am an educator
And pervasive human valor coconspirator
        I am in attrition
          I am in progression
           I am an amalgamation
             I am perfectly imperfect
              And imperfect perfectly
                I am a thesis of social injustice
                I am a vision of personal apotheosis
                I am all this and more...

I am        **ME!**

"All that I am, or hope to be, I owe to my angel mother.|"
Abraham Lincoln

# Exploring the Identity of an Iconoclastic Pioneer: My Mother

Haitian Women in Haiti are terribly oppressed, both economically and psychologically. I know this first hand, having grown up with five women in Haiti and observing their often delicate task of navigating in a sea of sharks: the male oppressors who limit them to being subservient and objectified. Having evolved from the roots of oppression, Haitian women are basking in their newfound freedom in America and they are growing out of the limitations once set on them in Haiti and branching out to achieve success and independence in this country. Yet still they have to deal with their former oppressors, the Haitian male who still refuses to see accept them in their new roles as heads of their own families, who at times ask to drive the cars that they pay for to drive them back and forth to work, even though the women are making the car payments. The oppressive Haitian male in America is experiencing a cultural shock to his outdated mentality of women at the bottom and men on top when it comes to the power structure that used to put women at a disadvantage in Haiti. My own mother has been approached many times by Haitian males who often proposition her to be their "woman" and by this I mean they want her to not only continue to work to take care of herself, but they also want her to make time to cook for them, wash their clothes, drive her back and for the to work in a car that *she* pays for while they stay home and watch tv and sneak other women to her bed while she's working to financially support them! And they are often surprised when my mother declines their offer. One even told her "I know why you don't want to be with me; you enjoy being free don't you? Because if you were to be with me, I would have to know your whereabouts every hour on the hour!"

which is the typical behavior of most Haitian males back in Haiti and even in America today! Some Haitian women tolerate this domineering behavior from the Haitian male in order to keep them in their lives. For some, their identities empty without the often suppressive presence of a man, any man. Even when enduring physical and psychological abuse, some woman prefer to stick by their man because they really believe, as they did in Haiti, that having a man is more acceptable to society then being single. They become more "respectable". Even if it costs them their freedoms. The extreme is emasculating the male so that females can empower themselves. In Haiti, there are narrow choices for Haitian women, but in America, wider choices are available to accommodate their yearnings of living independent of man and free themselves from the anchoring chains of subservience to reach ultimate levels of competency when making their aspirations a reality. To be endued with power, in America women have gained the temerity to challenge the limitations imposed on them by Haitian males; thus infringing on their civil rights and yearnings to pursue boundless happiness through their own personal achievements

Finally, Haitian women are reaping the rewards of acclimating to living in America. Essentially finding spiritual freedom and coming as close to social and economic equity as possible since leaving oppression in the form of economic and psychological misery in Haiti in search of equality in a mostly male dominated world. They are proving that they can be both iconoclastic and diplomatic in their torrid pursuit for justice, economic and social equity in the face of the officious male mentality. They have proven to be good communicators by being neither too passive nor overtly aggressive, but rightfully assertive. Some women are still so angry about having been oppressed by Haitian males in Haiti, that they have stopped dating them or limit their interactions with them all together. They have sought other ethnicities like Caucasian, Portuguese and so forth… The Haitian male in America still try to flex their dominating muscles on the Haitian woman who have reached a higher level of being by creating a life for themselves independent of the males, they have two or three jobs, are often home owners and entrepreneurs who also happen to be mothers, in Haiti being some man's wife and somebody's mother is usually their main identities, but in America, they have shed those restraints to explore other parts of themselves like innate desires to be take on leadership roles like pastors, artists, doctors, lawyers, engineers and last but not least, single mothers. They no longer feel the need to be trapped in bad marriages in order to have some sense of identity. Today in America, Haitian women are finding their truest identities outside of the unequivocal scorch of oppression from the Haitian male to live exhilarating lives that include but not limited to being mothers, breadwinners and essentially survivors!

"The leader has to be practical and a realist, yet must talk the language of the visionary and the idealist."

Eric Hoffer

# Exploring the Identity of an MIT Alumni: Community Visionary Johnny Monsarraton

Once upon a sunny day, I was strolling along my merry way... With autumn colors lighting up my path, the gentle breeze breathing kisses into my ears as I strolled along smiling through my fears. And then I came upon this gate, adorned with words encouraging me to accept my fate, giving me something to celebrate. It said "Your secret is that this powerless overwhelmed feeling is just a dream...Today is the day you awake... When you cross into the Abyss, with no path in sight, fearing one small change in your life may exhaust you entirely. When you believe and dare to proceed, your feet will find ground, new strength, more change and calm shores on the other side." And so I entered and then my journey began.

The following talk is with Johnny Monsarraton, the creator and founder of this awesome place he refers to as "a little shrine that looks a little like a Tibetan prayer wheel." I conducted this interview when I worked for Spare Change News.

Jacques Fleury: Tell me a bit more about who you are and what you do and how you do it. Elaborate on your life journey of self-discovery.

Johnny: I grew up in Massachusetts and was raised to believe in Big Projects. So in school I was always running student clubs – even playing the college mascot, the MIT Beaver -- and followed that up by starting a videogames company, Turbine, that's now the largest in New England. Along the way I learned a lot about life through my own problems. Most people follow their heart in love and their gut instinct for everything else. But I know my heart has led me astray and the head is much better at complex problems. So I recommend using your head, make a list, make a plan, work it out and don't give in to wishful thinking like "Maybe if I do nothing, it will get better".

JF: Why, when and how did you create and construct the concept for The Abyss? And where did you get the quote by the entrance?

Johnny: When I decided to turn my garden into a Big Project, I thought why not make it interactive? Why not include some of my life philosophy? I wrote the opening quote to inspire people to take action. The biggest obstacle to happiness is our fear of the future and this causes us to procrastinate on making the changes in our life we so desperately want. Basically, it's a garden. People enter and leave a card with a question in a submission box. I write an answer on the back of the card, and all the cards get posted in the garden in a little shrine that's looks a little like a Tibetan prayer wheel.

JF: Did you fund the project yourself or did you get some type of grant or donation? And who were the participants in helping to build this project? And how long did it take?

Johnny: It took 2 months to make it, and funded it myself. I was the only volunteer, although I paid some people to assist. Since the project opened in July, I've received $7 in donations. That's a pretty small amount, but each time I see that someone cares, it makes my day.

JF: What type of responses have you received on behalf of this project? How has it helped the community at large? Are you satisfied with the results or is there more that you'd like to see happen with this project?

Johnny: Everyone seems to love the concept, and people tell me that it's helped them to move past their fear of the future and actually take action. I'd like to think that my answers make sense, but even if they didn't – if it inspires people to get going, great. It's too much work to keep up forever, but if I can turn it into a regular newspaper column or a book I would like to keep going! I love adventures.

JF: How do you come up with the answers to the questions?

Johnny: I make the answers by empathizing with the question asker. That's why I take photographs for the website by putting each card on my refrigerator, like it's a second grader's art project. I care. Then I draw on my background and secular Big Project philosophy, and think, "How can I wake this person up and inspire him or her to action?" I spend over an hour a day on the Abyss, which is inspiring but also draining at times when I'm busy.

JF: Given the current state of the United States, (e.g. groundbreaking elections, partisan infighting, economic distress, contentious race relations etc...), how do you think something like The Abyss can affect the life of the people in your community and essentially the country at large?

Johnny: We like to think that only we alone have problems. But it's obvious coming to the garden, with the large shrine filled with questions, that we are not alone. Everyone has an issue on their mind, and being able to ask a question and see that somebody cares – even a stranger – seems to be uplifting to people.

JF: You may know of the movie with Kevin Spacey called "Pay It Forward", where one good deed triggers another good deed and so forth, do you think that there's any similarity between your philosophy and that of the movie and if yes how do you think you and/or the community can emulate the "pay it forward" ideology?

Johnny: I'm a big fan of the film, although I am wary of overinvestment. If you're so selfless that you're not taking care of yourself, it becomes unsustainable. This is why some people start to resent their obligations, even their jobs or children. So I think we should all be doing good deeds, but also finding a way to let these good deeds bring real joy into our lives, so we are benefiting as well. That's sustainable.

JF: In Haiti, I took it for granted that there was always a strong stable sense of "community". Our door was always open to visitors, neighbors etc... People would talk and visit with one another sporadically and no one ever passes you without greeting you and eye contact and an acknowledging smile or gesture was something that was intended and celebrated and not avoided and discouraged. I find that the exact opposite is true in most communities in Massachusetts. How do you think The Abyss can affect the community for the better and reduce the isolation felt by most in their respective communities?

Johnny: I hope the Abyss can give people a sense that somebody cares, they are not alone in having problems, and when someone writes a question about isolation, I encourage them to find a group. Cities have a different feel from rural areas, and I don't think Boston is especially different in that I can't greet each of the thousands of people I may pass on the street every day. People here have a huge drive to change the world, and the energy we don't give to strangers on the sidewalk we pour into our friendship community, our college community, our workplace community. So this idea of isolation is an illusion. You just have to find the right community and they're far more likely to have something in common with you than a stranger on the subway.

JF: Where do you go from here? Do you have any other philanthropic plans in the works?

Johnny: The person who organized the Boston Zombie March has moved to New York, and I would like to organize one for 2009. In this event, hundreds of people dressed in costume walk down the street – just for fun! – and I would like to revise the concept so that it's a charity walk and we are raising money for some benefit, possibly children's education. I'm also running a new startup company, Hard Data Factory. We supply event listings like concerts and theatre shows to newspapers and community Web sites.

JF: Having reviewed all the questions since The Abyss began, what has been your most favorite and poignant question and what was your response to it? And thank you for this interview.

Johnny: My very first question card, in jittery handwriting, said "I am afraid of life in it's ful essence, the future". I wrote back, "You are not alone… Make a plan to change your life. And the future won't be so unknown anymore."

# The Tree House: An Ode to My Father

"A father is a man who expects his son to be as good a man as he meant to be."

Frank A. Clark

While the butterfly hovers and the bird sways…
I take tepid steps around the forest
So not to disturb the natural way of things;
Night time in the woods,
I stroll into its evening with a lantern,
So dark a night I can only see what
The light will allow;
I can feel earthly debris crunching
Beneath my feet, the sounds echo in the distance,
I see the dilapidated treehouse that
Father and I built, a once buxom structure
Now barely standing with little nurturing…
Yet still I climb the ladder leading up to it,
The rungs creak beneath my feet,
I get into the pungent pad on the floor
And lay next to the spot where father
Once leisurely reposed while we talked into the night
Listening to at times tiresome benedictions:
The eternal noise of crickets and other cryptic night noises;
We spoke of traveling and transcending,
Navigating and never minding…
He spoke of his epistolary love with mother
And how they got together,
How glad he was when I saw light for the first time,
And how he would always be by my side,
"Promise?"

"Promise!"
"Cross your heart and hope to die?"
"Promise."
I can hear the leaves rustling in the wind,
As a gentle swaying of the treehouse that
Father and I built rocks me to sleep...

*"Strength does not come from winning. Your struggles develop your strengths. When you go through hardships and decide not to surrender, that is strength." --Arnold Schwarzenegger*

# And the Winner Is: How I Won an Award Just for Being My Authentic and Resilient Self

It had been two years since Center Club had its annual open house ceremonies due to the calamitous Covid19 pandemic. It is a time when staff, club members, family and friends congregate to celebrate the accomplishments of the members and acknowledge the diligent and compassionate support of the staff who help make it all possible. In this article, I will recount my journey to Center Club on the path to winning the Seth Pope Employment Award for my entrepreneurship as an author, guest speaker and certified private tutor with my business listed on Staples Connect directory of local small businesses.

I first met executive director Mary Gregorio when I first came to Center Club as a graduate student of Human Services and Family Development for Tufts University. By that point, I had already completed a degree in Liberal Arts from the University of Massachusetts and was at the cusp of writing for mainstream print and online news media. In the past, I had been a member of the editing staff of literary magazines and newspapers in both high school and college. First I was student editor in chief of Boston English High School's *EXPRESSIONS* and head writer for the school newspaper (for which I received a scholarship and the journalism award upon graduation) and a member of the editing staff of *Watermark*, a literary magazine at the University of Massachusetts, Boston.

What I had learned about Center Club then was that it is the oldest and largest Clubhouse in New England for people afflicted with various forms of atypical brains. The club has an assiduity to the doctrines of self-help, peer support and empowerment. The initial stages of the club revert to 1958, when co-founder Dr. Sam Grob, began meeting with six freshly discharged patients. They gathered in the headquarters of the Massachusetts Association of Mental Health with the purpose of forming a "friendship club."

Now years later here I am, once an intern and now a member of such an iconic establishment where making "friendships" or supportive connections are paramount. It took a harrowing journey to get here, after years of ups and downs in and out of hospitals, schools, colleges and workplaces. There isn't sufficient space in this script to go into the details, trust me! However, my point is I *persevered* along with the support of my family and friends, but especially my mother, who was at the Open House on November 3rd, 2022 in a definitive show of support. She saw me through dropping in, out and in again in Massachusetts area colleges and Universities and losing and gaining employment over the course of many years. Unfortunately, early on after being diagnosed, I had a therapist who told me that my prognosis was not going to be a good one. He said that in his "experience", he had seen patients like myself get worse, not better. Feeling nonplussed and resolved to prove him wrong, I worked and worked and worked some more until before his very eyes, he saw me publishing my first Boston Globe featured book: *Sparks in the Dark: A Lighter Shade of Blue, A Poetic Memoir* about my personal journey—which was much like an indiscernible amorphous cloud mass—to recovery. Today, I have received a business school diploma, completed two college certificate programs and received an undergraduate college degree, I currently spearhead my own business as a College of Reading and Learning Association Certified Tutor in English composition, writing coach and guest speaker as a published author of four books and included as a contributing writer in .eight literary anthologies. I am also taking professional development classes in the literary arts from Harvard University online in an effort to achieve a Masters of Fine Arts in Creative Writing and Creative Non-Fiction, hoping to whet my craft as an author and entrepreneur.

As you can see, my journey to receiving the Seth Pope Employment Award was winding, with no clear path to the apex of success. Nevertheless, I persevered with the support of my family, friends and community crusaders like Center Club who persevered right alongside me to make this monumental moment in my life possible. I saw a commercial with a young female basketball player talking about when you receive an award, no matter whose name is on it, it's essentially a TEAM award. Hence, even if it's my name on the plaque, I dedicate it to all who made it possible! My work has just begun, for I can't rest on my laurels just because I received an award, if anything, it's a motivator to keep going, succeeding and sharing the fruits of my labor with my supportive family and community. In the coming years, Center Club members will hopefully see much more of me and I will continue to value their wisdom and support and give back in any way that I can to an iconic organization that has given me so much. I won an award just for being whom I was meant to be and to that end, you too can win or continue to win if you find and follow your own light that highlights your most authentic self.

# Scribbles

## La vie

Ah, la douleur de la vie;
So sorrowful this life can be,
We live in a constant that is uncertainty,
Waiting to awaken in morning can be tiresome,
Waking from a nightmare can be winsome,
'Til we see the dreadful daylight of reality!
Yearning to sleep;
Daring to wake;
What comes next?
Life is but a haste!

## Bird Bath

The mockingbird emerged from its bath,
Singing while it sat on a raft,
Looking into the distant path,
And poised with some sass,
Swiftly flew off in a fit of wrath!

## Insomnia

I dreamed I had insomnia
And birds of prey roamed
'Round my sphere
My heart rhythm's tachycardia
Abided in a bed of fear…

I dreamt I slept with insomnia
echoes of children
Resounded like nostalgia
My senses somewhat forlorn

Yearning for the years bygone
Wishing to wish away my melancholia

I dream of sleep
Awake I weep
I dreamt i prayed
My soul to keep
I fell asleep
Or so it seems
Wishing to weep
For my esteem
Alas to sleep
per chance to dream…

## *What Place is This?*

Surrounded by a shadowy grey environ,
Sitting cross legged on some ground,
Looking up in a circular motion,
I wondered why there was no one else around…
Yearning to hear a sound;
Something has blurred my vision,
Suddenly I hear a pound,
Could thunder be a thing I found?!
Alas…The dawning of my wakening,
I am living in a cloud!!!

"I have come to believe that a great teacher is a great artist and there as few as any other great artists. Teaching might even be the greatest of the arts since the medium is the human mind and spirit."

John Steinbeck

# Lessons Learned: What Every Student Needs in Their Classrooms

## An Ode to My Inspirational Writing Teacher from America's first High School

It is with great fervor and honor that I write about Mr. Powers, my favorite English teacher from the oldest public school in America, Boston English High School (est. 1821).

Every student should have a "Mr. Powers" in his/ her/ or their lives! I remember the first time I met him with lapidary clarity. It was at the confluence of my experiences as a bilingual student and the ensuing culture clash having immigrated to America from Haiti. He was sitting down when I walked into his classroom. He looked up with a sort of wild eyed mystic, full of wisdom and truth and a rather refreshing informal disposition. The sun seeping from the glass window made his dirty blond hair shimmer, rendering it nearly golden. I came to proffer my candidacy as a writer for the EHS literary magazine "IMPRESSIONS" at the request of my journalism teacher & editor of the school newspaper Mrs. Halloran, if I remember her name correctly… After introductions, I handed him a sample of a story I had written. He snatched it with gusto and curiosity and began perusing it immediately.

I stood before him, my heart thudding as if with analogous intensity of a bird's rapid heart rate. I thought that if THIS was how it felt to anticipate being judged for my writing, was I really ready!? Sure I had been judged for my journalism writings, but that was different, that was just an amalgamation of facts and academic forms. THIS, however, was my heart on a piece of paper, an esoteric construction of my imagination and my hitherto life observations and nascent wisdom. After he was done, he glanced up at me with a resolute smile and I just knew that he was going to let me have it! But then again, particularly back then as a mostly melancholy teen, I anticipated the worst in life. He said, "Are you serious about becoming a writer?" and I said, "Yes" without any hesitation. "Ok then, can I be totally honest with you? I shook my head 'Yes'. 'Some students break into tears on me, YOU won't, will you?" And I shook my head "NO" without flinching. Then he sat me down, and red marked my story to death! One word in particularly stayed in my mind until this day...he wrote "TRITE TRITE TRITE!!!" all over my work. Apparently I was using an overabundance of what he considered to be banal language that permeated my script. He felt that I should make my works my own, and use words that "wake-up" the reader rather than subdue them with monotonous circumlocution or verbosity. I became genuinely intrigued by his wild eyed earnest honesty, he was like a mad literary scientist, full of efficacious ideas and suggestions, and I couldn't take notes fast enough.

After that encounter, we began working together regularly after school, he published my stories in IMPRESSIONS and we developed a mutual respect for each other. He selected me among a handful of students to represent English High along with the Boston Latin School in a two-week summer literary seminar at Andover Academy in Andover, Massachusetts; which culminated to the participants publishing a literary magazine and giving a public reading for faculty and family. The magazine had three titles: "IMPRESSIONS/No Repression of Expression/In Our Own Write".

Then Mr. Powers bestowed upon me the highest honor any bilingual student had hitherto received, making me editor-in-chief of IMPRESSIONS. Because of his demonstrated belief in me, I became emboldened in my pursuit of a career in writing. After high school, I was on the editing staff of the literary magazine 'The Watermark' at

University of Massachusetts, Boston. I have since had and still have columns in a number of newspapers and magazines, my first book "Sparks in the Dark" was featured in the Boston Globe and I have published three books total, second one being a fiction collection titled It's Always Sunrise Somewhere and Other Stories' the latest being 'Chain Letter To America: The One Thing You Can Do To End Racism, A Collection of Essays, Fiction and Poetry Celebrating Multiculturalism" which is sold at the Harvard Book Store in Cambridge, Massachusetts and online. I have also been included in seven anthologies, one of which from Cornell University Press in New York and London, England.

I owe a generous debt of gratitude to Mr. Powers for his tough talking, disciplined & inspiring methods that helped propelled me to the literary and life success that I enjoy today. THANK YOU MR. POWERS, wherever you are….

# Capital vs. People

Be careful where you place your value;
Because when you place your value
On *capital* over *people*,
Remember, capital cannot visit you
When you're in the *hospital*...

"Black men struggle with masculinity so much. The idea that we must always be strong really presses us all down - it keeps us from growing."
Donald "Childish Gambino" Glover

# TOUGH: Exploring the Contentious Issue of Masculinity in Contemporary Society

As a child, my mother often painted my fingernails and sent me to school with glossy lips and lavishly perfumed hands. So began my confusing journey in discovering my gender identity and tipping along the jagged edges of sexual non-conformity.

Gender, as defined in *Down to Earth Sociology*, is "The social expectations attached to a person on account of that person's sex. Sex is biological while gender is social."

It has occurred to me that sexual and gender identity has been a hot-tempered issue most recently. People are quick to use labels like Gay, Straight, and Bisexual, Queer, Transgender, Feminine, Masculine, Macho, Tough Guy and Snowflake. Essentially, if you're labeled gay then, you're thought of as feminine and if considered straight, then you're thought of as masculine. Well, if only it was all that simple.

Eli Coleman, in his book *Integrated Identities for Gay Men and Lesbians* states that "The dichotomous or trichotomous categories of sexual orientation (homosexual, heterosexual, bisexual) are a massive over simplification of our current understanding of sexual orientation." He goes on to day that "…conflicts within or between individuals over sexual orientation are quite commonly seen in many cases of individual psychopathology. These conflicts contribute to psychosexual dysfunctions, relational problems, career indecision …existential crisis and so forth." I remember the anxiety I experienced when I decided to become a male nurse; I worried about the implications of working in a field typically dominated by woman. But as we know today, there are many male nurses whose sexual identities are exclusively heterosexual, even though they have taken on a mostly feminine role and ignored the gender (masculine or feminine) role expectations of society. Coleman also quoted Alfred Kinsey—a pioneer in the area of human sexuality research, whose 1948 publication "Sexual Behavior in the Human Male" was one of the first recorded works that saw science address sexual behavior and who invented the "Kinsey Scale" that rates levels of sexual preference from 1 (absolutely straight) to 6 (absolutely gay)—as saying "The world is not divided into sheeps and goats. Not all are black nor all are white. The living world is a continuum in each and every one of its aspects. The sooner we learn this concerning human sexual behavior, the sooner we shall reach a sounder understanding of the realities of sex."

"Masculinity is what you believe it to be. I think masculinity and femininity is something that's very old-fashioned. There's a whole new generation of people who aren't defined by their sex or race or who they like to sleep with." Asserted gay Olympic Gold Medalist Johnny Weir and rightfully so…. In the grand scheme of things, I think that new age sexuality borders on being more contextual than it is biological. There have been times when one can feel attracted to someone based on the situation of which they find themselves and the feelings that develop during that time; taking into consideration that they may still have more feelings of physical attract toward one sex over the other. Attraction can be more than just wanting to have intercourse with someone. It can be a combination of things that one deems valuable when it comes to finding the right mate. Things like karma, aura, emotional chemistry, intellectual and spiritual compatibility and socioeconomic components; all can affect attraction among individuals.

As a matter of fact, when I was growing up with my male cousin Bob in Haiti, definitive distinctions were made between us in relation to our disparate levels of gender role conformity.

Growing up, I was extremely close to my mother and had limited contact with my father being that he was a traveling businessman who lived in the second floor living quarters of his retail store in the middle of the city of Port-au-Prince. I was seen as the soft spoken, non-aggressive, overly sensitive and not terribly athletic mama's boy. Whereas my cousin Bob was perceived to be the more tough talking, boisterous, athletic, and insensitive man's man. So they invented names to "label" us. I was "Temou" (Creole for soft core) and he was "Tedi" (Creole for hard core). Those labels began to shape how I perceived myself in the early stages of my psychological development. The idea that to be masculine you must be boisterous, not soft spoken is part of the pathology behind the idea of masculinity. "Violence has always been unfortunately embedded in masculinity, this alpha thing." Said *Captain America* star Sebastian Stan.

Robert J. Stoller, M.D., in his book *Presentations of Gender* talks about the issue of femininity and masculinity in boys and girls within the context of family dynamics. He states that "One might hypothesize that if an excessively close mother child symbiosis and a distant and passive father produce extreme femininity in males, [then] too little symbiosis with the mother and too much symbiosis with the father would produce very masculine females." Which brings me to pose this question: Why are we as man so afraid to be associated with acting or thinking "like a girl"? What's wrong with acting or thinking like a girl? We are all made of both male and female chromosomes, right? Sometimes the female chromosomes (a female karyotype is 46 XX) can be more dominant in males and the male chromosomes (a male karyotype is 46 XY) can be more dominant in females and vice versa. Speaking from the point of view of someone who grew up with about five dominant women who exhibited both feminine and masculine characteristics in Haiti, I've grown to have immense respect for women and their abilities to communicate, empathize, endure and thrive over hardships. Why are those qualities recognized as a source of weakness if exhibited in males? Women tend to allow themselves to be emotionally vulnerable, whereas men tend to perceive vulnerability as a weakness. But why is that? It seems to me that it takes *courage* and *strength* to be vulnerable whereas it takes *fear* and *weakness* to be invulnerable. In Haiti, women are objectified and are made to be subservient to men. So the strong woman I grew up with, had to mask their strengths or what was perceived to be masculine traits in order to appease the men, or risked being labeled a lesbian and lose their breadwinner. As for me, at times I had to act like the typically stoical masculine male when I really felt like sobbing uncontrollably, in order to avoid being labeled a sissy.

In "The Homosexualities: Reality, Fantasy, and the Arts", Shirley Panken, Ph.D. writes "In Virginia Wolf's celebrated essay 'A Room of One's Own', Woolf…[discredits] the usual definition of masculinity and femininity, and synchronizes the two into an androgynous (genderless) vision." She goes on to say that in Wolf's other work "Orlando", she "depicts Orlando's profound confusion about the diversity of his/her different selves." Woolf writes that the indecision "from one sex to another is universal, that clothing may depict male or female likeness, but that underneath the sex, is opposite of what is above. She also dwells on the multiplicity of the self…"

Consequently, I want all the "feminine" or non-stereotypically "masculine" men out there to unite and claim their gender bending rights! Roy Simmons, a former offensive lineman with the New York Giants and with the Super Bowl winning Washington Redskins in the 1980s and the second NFL player to come out as gay, in a book about him called *Out of Bounds* had this to say: "To me, I am and always have been Roy Simmons. Labels are for people trying to define me—that's *their* problem. The only insight I can offer into my sexuality is that I did exactly what everybody else around me did when I was growing up: when I came into my sexual maturity, I went with the flow, and for me the flow moved naturally to boys *and* girls. I found out soon that I like dick and pussy in almost equal measure—you don't need a label to enjoy either one. A label is for the outside trying to look in." Recently, a large number of stereotypically "masculine" men have come out as Gay, Bisexual or Transgender, like former Gold Medal Winning decathlete Caitlyn Jenner born Bruce Jenner. During his last 20/20 interview with Diane Sawyer back on April 24th, 2015 before he transitioned to

Caitlyn Jenner, Sawyer asked him about his sexuality and to which he replied, "Sexuality is who you go to bed with, gender is who you go to bed as…" Among other high profile "masculine" athletes who have come out as gay or bisexual to challenge the contentious ideologies of masculinity are:

Carl Nassib, who became the first active National Football League (NFL) player to come out as gay. Luke Prokop, who became the first NHL player to come out as gay. Michael Sam was the first openly gay man drafted into the NFL. Ryan Russell became the first openly bisexual person in the NFL and in any major professional league. Ryan O'Callaghan who came out as gay after retiring from the NFL. John Amaechi who came out as gay in 2007, four years after retiring from the National Basketball Association (NBA). Glenn Burke became the first gay man in the Major League Baseball (MLB). Robbie Rogers was the first openly gay soccer player in a professional league. Jason Collins was the NBA's first openly gay player. Meanwhile, Orlando Cruz became the first openly gay man in boxing and Darren Young in wrestling. The list goes on and on…see it in full with this link:

https://www.insider.com/professional-athletes-who-are-lgbt

In contemporary society, it is becoming increasingly unacceptable for men to objectify women. The days of "cat calling" (e.g. Wolf whistle, "Hey baby, can I get your number?", "Nice ass!" etc…) is becoming passé. In addition, when it comes to having sexual explorative freedom, the double standard of toadying men and shaming women has also been exposed and reassessed.

All of this and more are part of the concepts of masculinity: what it means to be a "real man." Today, a plethora of men are redefining their own manhood and not simply acquiescing to pre-established and progressively antiquated prototypes of masculinity. Terminologies like "house husbands" and "stay-at-home dads" are part of newfangled lexicon. Today's men tend to be more expressive about their feelings and famous men like the comedian and actor Chris Rock has admitted to going to therapy.

In a *People Magazine* article by Eric Todisco titled: "Chris Rock Reveals He Does Seven Hours of Therapy a Week Since Onset of COVID-19 Pandemic" published on Dec. 10, 2020. Todesco writes that Rock unbosomed himself to the Hollywood Reporter about his therapy, revealing that he has been focusing on rectifying "childhood traumas".

"I thought I was actually dealing with it, and the reality is I never dealt with it," Rock stated.

Hence as you can see, it is becoming incrementally acceptable for men to find ways to cope with their feelings, which most of them (me included) were told they should *not* have or must *not* show. Alternatively, it is no longer acceptable to use coping patterns like drinking, drugging, physical violence and abusing women and children. To do so now will result in official consequences due to new and better-implemented domestic violence laws.

Today, you need not behave like a galoot with a "cave man" mentality to affirm your masculinity. Violence and intimidation—both archetypally associated with masculinity—are not "strengths"; they are personal weaknesses. As Argentinian revolutionary writer George Louis Borges once said, "Violence is the last resort of the weak." Some of the strongest men in history did not use force and fear to exert their masculinity. Iconoclasts like Gandhi, Nelson Mandela and Dr. Martin Luther King Jr. changed the world through non-violent means. It is easier to react violently like an unruly toddler than it is to respond thoughtfully like a mature man. Therefore, for those of you who are questioning your gender identity (masculinity, femininity) and sexuality (lesbian, gay, straight, bisexual, transsexual, queer, intersexed, asexual and questioning), know that the only one who can define you is *you*. Do not allow *external* forces keep you from experiencing *internal* freedom, whether you identify as masculine, feminine or both! After all, what is more divine than knowing both masculine and feminine energies?

# *ReXsume*

| | |
|---|---|
| Objective: | Seeking a position to be over, under or next to someone;<br>Willing to fill any opening or position… |
| Education: | Certificate of participation in "group" activities |
| Experience: | Been around the block a few times… |
| Skills: | Can touch my lower stomach *without* using my hands |
| Achievements: | Never been arrested for se**X** crimes |
| Hobbies: | All things done in the dark |
| References: | See attached list for numbers of *satisfied* customers! |

"All the world's a stage, and all the men and women merely
players: they have their exits and their entrances; and one man
in his time plays many parts, his acts being seven ages."

William Shakespeare

# PART III
## The Arts

# *Folk Song*

*Inspired by the love between Lisa and Dave of the neo-folk group Sweet Wednesday*
*Who turned my poems into songs in our CD "A Lighter Shade of Blue"…*

Speak to me like a singer sings a folk song,
so i can close my eyes and see infinity
pure beauty like
hazy
    lazy
        rays
             of late summer slicing through the forest trees
echos of children full of merriment tumbling on green pastures over hillsides
            the greenest greens i've ever seen
like seeing life in  s l o w
          m o t i o n
speak to me like
a singer sings a love song
with sweet tongued melodies and harmonies
        to break the morning    dawn
with coffee brewing and your smile like a kiss across the distant bay
wind whistles like a winded breath sounding the wind chimes
    hanging
        from our front porch
overlooking our vast terrain animated with farm animals and insects
that make night music by bonfires as we hold our cups of southern comfort
       and speak of dreams long dead and gone with little time left
to dream anew listening to crickets chirp in secret monotonous lullabies
       and the moon hovers over like our halo
       with us by each other's sides    we're good
              to

**g**

     **o**

wherever we may go
even in the hereafter i still yearn to hear you
     speak in songs of drealike sounds like sonatas
you'll strum your guitar and open your mouth
both no longer emit a           sound
but even your soundless voice amuses me
and beyond the border that hovers between life and death
I sit by you with a ghostly grin and listen to you     sing

like you talk
     like a folk song...

"In age of consumerism and materialism, I traffic in blue sky and colored air."

James Turrell

## *Exploring the Arts: Nothing "Blue" About Blue Man Group*

In a world maligned by socio-political division, our society is most definitely overzealous for something to mitigate its intermittent malaise.

Then comes Blue Man Group: an American Performance Art Company founded in 1987; like a fast moving storm, boldly rushes into The Charles Playhouse to strut their wildly colorful rapid-fire Ritalin paced show! The Canadian Company Cirque Du Soleil purchased the company in 2017. The show, which was surprisingly interactive, started out with the audience following the directions of a scrolling marquee. The audience was engaged in reading the words out loud which was meant to be like a warm up before the Blue Man made their blue appearance. Another thing, which stroked me as peculiar, was that the first three rows of people were wearing raincoats. I must admit, since I was in a suit, I experienced some minor anxiety not knowing what was going to happen. All I could think of was the performance artist "Gallagher" smashing watermelons to wet his audience's appetite for a meticulously planned mess. Toward the middle of the one hour and forty-five minute show, the Blue Man squirted banana juice all over the eager audience! Interpret that as you wish!

Essentially, the show had the flare of a circus with something for everyone! It was what I would call edu-tainment, a mixture of education and entertainment. At one point, it became philosophical by encouraging us to appreciate the here and now instead of worrying about what's coming up next. Then on the other hand it was engaging when the Blue Men picked a female audience member, brought her up on stage and strapped a blue-breasted suit on her. Their comedic talents became evident when all they did for a few minutes was just sit there behind a table all aligned in a row and stared while their "victim" masquerading as their date waited patiently for the Blue boys next move. Eventually they began to interact with her by playing romantic music, setting flowers on the table and sharing their "Twinkies" (described as a finger shaped cake filled with white cream) with her. Again, interpret that as you wish! Then in a disgusting twist, the newly digested Twinkies turned into yellow liquid and began to pour out of their chests, which emanated a drone of disgust from the audience.

All in all, the Blue Men were innovative and alluring. They even parodied what they call "The new Rock 'n Roll" band as a bunch of choreographed boy bands who eventually disband to break out into their separate "projects" when they reach their height of success as a group. In doing this, they demonstrated their versatility as performers, gyrating their limber bodies to dance music. I was particularly pleased with their drumming, a sound that penetrating my pores so that the drum beats became synonymous with my own heartbeat. The finale had pounding dance music and rolls of white toilet paper falling from the ceiling in a white fluorescent light reaching a crescendo of climatic proportions! Everyone was on their feet, saturated in a creamy white glow and giggling like children during recess on the playground.

Then the Blue Men even waited in the lobby for picture opportunities and signed autographs with blue paint. The audience, a mixture of the young and the young at heart, left beaming from ear to ear. And that's why the Blue Men are here in Boston to turn our moods from "blue" to blissful and for a brief moment, forget about our woe and foster a sense of unity and camaraderie in spite of our disparate identities.

"Life is a dream for the wise, a game for the fool, a comedy for the rich, a tragedy for the poor."

Sholom Aleichem

## Exploring the Arts: Resilient Women Dreaming Big in the Movie "Dream Girls"

"Dream Girls" reigned as a rip roaring; nail biting; brink of your seat extravaganza; a fantastic spectacular oasis of a movie! And that's only the beginning.

Bill Condon's adaptation of Tom Eyen & Henry Krieger's 25-year-old Broadway musical rushed into theatres like a tornado to, as one critic puts it, "Save a lackluster Fall." And a heavy dose of luster and glamour they brought to the big screen to an eager audience. However, not everyone are singing their praises.

Because there has been a plethora of effusive exaltations for "Dream Girls", I became curious to read some of the less sycophantic comments. One critic said: "...the reviews are in, and after listening to the ...praise[s], I'm ready to belt out the following show stopper: 'I Ain't Addin' My Voice to this Choir, No HOW!" He goes on to describe Beyonce as "ineffective", Jamie Foxx as "constipated", Eddie Murphy as resorting to reiterating his SNL-era James Brown routine and the movie's "utter failure to capture the Motown Sound." The picture's only saving grace, he says, is American Idol looser Jennifer Hudson "...bellowing the crowd-pleasing 'And I'm Telling You I'm Not Going'."

Basically here you have a case of what I call the "Cynical Critic Syndrome." After all, a critic's job is to criticize. And most often panning a movie can be much more fun to read than syrupy praises. So

I don't blame him for doing what's expected of him. However, I have to disagree with him.

The movie was exceptionally entertaining with its lush costumes, majestic set decorations and a believable plot. The vitality and circumstances of the actors kept the audience on a tight rope trajectory that navigated between triumph and failure, taking us on a musical roller coaster that we never wanted to end. Jennifer Hudson did not go unnoticed as she delivered a thunderstorm of a performance, commanding our attention every time she emerged on screen. I noticed that some audience members leaning forward upon her presence. Of course since the Hudson character "Effie" played the underdog, everyone seemed to be rooting for her. The Beyonce character "Deena" played the reluctant villain and seen as culpable for Effie's downfall. Her performance, however, took a back seat to Hudson's more impassioned and compelling persona. The Jamie Foxx Character was more vitriolic than "constipated", since he was modeled after recording mogul Barry Gordy, who was responsible for the rise of *The Supremes*, of whom the movie is loosely based on.

The movie was a tale of bravery and sacrifice, love and loss, failure and ultimately success! The intrepid Effie embodied the full burden of disobedience with magnificent elegance, as she fervently treaded shark-infested waters. She was on a balance beam of power and powerlessness as she finds herself in an industry dominated by merciless men. She endured unfathomable cruelty and injustice with a remarkable combination of innocence and maturity; vulnerability and strength as she continually adjust to the unjust and re-adjust to the hurls of fire that life constantly threw at her. She is our modern day heroine. The audience cheered in her triumph over adversity.

Murphy lived up to his usual comical trademark as a drug addicted singer who likes to "...shake things up." He managed to escape the curse of his one and only hit "Party All the Time" back in the 1980's by delivering strong svelte vocal performances. The film also touched base on the issues of race and conformity in the music industry in examining what is considered "acceptable" for a black musician to crossover to a predominantly white audience.

This movie has Golden Globe written all over it! It appears as if the "Dream Girls" took a fictional pledge to be FABULOUSLY entertaining and I think they more than delivered. And to those with the "Cynical Critic Syndrome", I believe there's a new cure for that, it's called Milk of Magnesia. Got Milk?

"We're born alone, we live alone, we die alone. Only through our love and friendship can we create the illusion for the moment that we're not alone."

Orson Welles

# Exploring the Arts: A Meditation on Romantic Love at Lyric Stage's "The Last Five Years"

"Take a breath, take a step, take a chance" declares Jared Troilo as "Jamie" in the Lyric Stage Company's Boston production of "The Last Five Years." Written and composed by Jason Robert Brown and directed by Leigh Barret in this musical drama.

This play tells the story of a couple who fell in and out of love over the course of five years. Interestingly enough, the leading characters are played by real life husband and wife team Jared (Jamie) and Kira (Cathy) Troilo—who have known each other since grade school. The narrative is told paradoxically as "Cathy" recounts her journey looking back on what happened, whereas "Jamie" accounts for *his* version looking forward, which in itself can be a metaphor for how some of us choose to navigate our lives, living in the past or mindfully living for the present.

"In 'The Last Five Years', Cathy is lamenting an ending, while Jamie is celebrating a beginning." Explains Lyric Stage executive and artistic directors Matt Chapuran and Courtney O'Connor. They relate this story to our immanent reality seemingly entombed in sociopolitical and public health crises in the form of the Covid19 pandemic. "This certainly feels like all of us right now: peering out into the world once again [after Covid lockdowns] eager to embrace the best…of the future, but doing so with the knowledge of our past shortcomings…"

Whether it's navigating the world as it shifts around us, or navigating our personal lives as we fall in and out of love with our prospective companions, *Last Five Years* can be interpreted as a symbol of contemplation for what makes things go right as well as what makes them go abysmally wrong. It does so while utilizing simple staging with discernible pulchritude akin to the sparkly newness often at the onset of most romantic relationships. The singing was at times ethereal, particularly from "Cathy" at her most agonizing moments and a permeation of tender melancholia was present towards the end encompassing both characters which was rendered quite effectively in their heartfelt singing. The spinning of the stage could serve to symbolize how life can spin and shift at any moment and we have the opportunity to see it from a different perspective.

Much like life, director Leigh Barret describes the play as "…a beautiful complicated mess." It proffers us the opportunity to learn something about the way we communicate or miscommunicate, perceive or misperceive each other which can lead to misunderstandings that can result in permanently damaged or ultimately severed relationships, romantic or otherwise. It puts forth the idea that in any relationship, we have a chance to make "…discoveries about communication, awareness, acknowledgement, and the value of grace… [or forgiveness]" according to Barret. This I see as an effective methodology to move forward rather than backwards while navigating life's turntable of joys and woes.

If you have a penchant for musicals and are also a romantic, or paradoxically if you're a skeptic of both, then this terrific little slice of life just might sing its way into your heart and change your mind.

"One of the penalties of refusing to participate in politics is that you end up being governed by your inferiors."

Plato

# Exploring The Arts: Sweat Posits Race, Class & Friendship at the Huntington:

*Tackling political, racial and class divisions in Trump Era America*

"We will not continue to bear our backs for them to strike us down!" Exclaims one of the characters in two-time Pulitzer Prize winning African American Brown and Yale University graduate and Columbia University professor Lynn Nottage's excoriating and unmistakably timely Pulitzer Prize winning play *Sweat* directed by Kimberly Senior at the Huntington Avenue Theatre in Boston and extended by popular demand from Jan. 31 through Mar. 1, 2020.

This searing production is about a group of working class friends and co-workers in Reading, Pennsylvania navigating their relationships amidst the pitfalls of corporate downsizing as factories either shut down or initiate the harrowing process of trimming their employees due to robots replacing humans consequential to, mostly and pejoratively, greedy white American patriarchal fat cat's hungry aspirations for profit proliferation. The multiracial cast speaks to imminent racial and sociopolitical divisions in America and even beyond as matters of religion, immigration and economic inequity galvanizing friends to turn against one another as focal points of blame resulting from disenfranchising and disadvantageous institutional policies affecting the bottom feeders of our society, coming from uppermost political hierarchies in the echelons of those bearing the lambasted breadth of institutional power.

*Sweat* speaks to the issues that divide us in Trump Era America with ruthless and unrepentant honesty, a vivid sociopolitical theatrical avatar of the frail facade of the human condition fundamentally—although clumsily, transcending our inexorable foibles to emerge victorious even in spite of ourselves. The production creates a realistic atmosphere with believable staging and true to life characters that one can immediately recognize and relate to. The story is told using a flash-back and flash-forward effect, that I found to be sometimes somewhat confounding, but one can still manage to follow the plot with relative ease and clarity. Controversial issues like Black History Month is brought up when a white character bellows "Make white people feel guilty month...[and] Why don't we have a white history month?" and one liners like "They don't even see you...you think they give a damn about your black *ss?"

The play raises questions about race, class, friendships and family and rightfully without providing immediate answers, as is the responsibility of effective art to raise questions and allows the audience to come to their own conclusions. Essentially and despite our differences, *Sweat* sends one clear message: that our collective "humanity is at the core of everything..." and I couldn't agree more. See it and you be the judge.

I give this profound production a five out of five stars!

# Exploring the Arts: Witch Casts Just the Right Spell (or Does She?)

"I'm like a disease that only I seem to have caught…" begins a jarring introductory soliloquy from Elizabeth Sawyer, the principal character from *Witch* as played by prolific Boston based actress Lyndsay Allyn Cox. Written by New York based playwright Jen Silverman and directed by Boston local Rebecca Bradshaw, this production is playing at the Huntington Theater's Calderwood Pavilion/Boston Center for the Arts from Oct. 15th to Nov. 14th, 2021.

"Elizabeth," a single woman presumed to be a "Witch" lives in what is described as a country village in Edmonton. Amidst navigating a life of persecution and vitriol saunters in "Scratch" who is the devil incarnate as played by Michael Underhill, who previously appeared in the Huntington's production of *Man in the Ring* back in 2018. He proffers to her an opportunity for "revenge" against her tormentors in exchange for her soul, nonplused and intrigued by her leery propensity to not readily yield to his protracted cajoling (particularly since some other members of the town folk have already become ensnared in his trap in exchange for their souls). This essentially marks the starting point of interest in this mordant play for the scenarios that resulted out of what could have been a predictable afflicted witch revenge story turned into a complex tale of forbidden love, lust, gender biases, challenging systemic inequality and emphasizing ideologies of "the other" in our society and daring to challenge the status quo of the power structures that has defined our lives for centuries.

"The character of Elizabeth is forcing you to look at the status quo and question it," explained *Witch* director Rebecca Bradshaw in an interview with Huntington production dramaturg Pascale Florestal. She went on to say, "That is so important right now, to not get stuck in our own ways or in societal ways and to really think about why we do the things we do." Ponderings that have become even more pressing during the pandemic inertia while the world was in quarantine.

Playwright Jen Silverman echoes Bradshaws's assertions that "…the question of transformation, whether or not we are capable of change, how far people will go to feel visible, to be perceived the way they want to be perceived…how we get trapped by systemic power dynamics [and] what it takes to break free."

This is the first play I've seen since the 2020 Covid pandemic hiatus of well, EVERYTHING, but for this purpose, particularly the arts. Amidst challenging times like these, I truly believe that the arts proffers creative altruistic opportunities to be a guiding light in immanent darkness, a beacon of hope in all worldly madness. *Witch* sets the stage, granted it's a stage rightfully full of questions but also lays out ample opportunities to decipher a plethora of possible answers.

Right from the onset, *Witch* casts its spell and snatches our attention with a bold and foreboding soliloquy from principle character Elizabeth as the witch. As she delivered her inauspicious speech, she radiated confidence, authority and control and I, for one, readily surrendered to Madame "Witch" and with marked accelerated heart rate—due to a fair amount of trepidation—was willing to go wherever she saw fit to take me.

One of the most important characteristics of the theater is the ability to be pliable, to shift and reflect what is happening in a precise moment in time. Although this play was written in 2018, it still manages to be relevant in 2021 since we are still facing some of the same afflictions from 2018. The pandemic is still lingering on with Covid19 "variants" morphing into other more deadly "variants," remnants of a precarious political climate since the contentious election of Joe Biden. There is still much social unrest due to a panoramic number of issues ranging from America's reckoning with racial justice and gender gaps to abortion rights and rainbow flag communities all fighting for unequivocal equality. *Witch* becomes a buxom motif for "the other" in a society where not all are necessarily created equal. The fact that Elizabeth as the witch is played by a woman of color, a black woman in particular, was not lost on me.

Elizabeth explains how she doesn't feel "seen," how people make uncorroborated claims about her character simply because she's been labeled a "witch," much like some people make uncorroborated assertions about those who have been labeled "black" simply because they are black. Even though this play is based on the 1621 Jacobean era original play *The Witch of Edmonton: A Tragic Comedy* by William Rowley et al, it still manages to be relevant in contemporary times, underscoring our prejudices against each other, whether conscious or subconscious. It is a grievous reminder that treating some like "the other" is not a present day anachronism that should have been left in the past. It is a present day reality that we as a society ARE constantly railing against so that it does not become the legacy we leave behind for our posterity.

Smart effective staging that weaved in and out as if seamlessly, casting that could only be compared to a strike of lightning hitting the same place twice, and a deliciously contrasting tension of the erotic and the demonic sort between the characters, mostly due to a devilishly handsome devil stirring the pot that will ignite towns peoples' stealthy passions and desires.

Although the staging resembled 17th century England with a Jacobean décor, the dialogue is modern, fresh and sometimes caustic without any "fake" English accents per the request of the playwright. One particular moment of modern dialogue that brought delight and laughter from the audience was when Elizabeth boldly tells the devil that he's been "talking sh★t" just to give you an idea.

This production is a bewitching Risorgimento wailing for an apocalyptic end to the status quo in a manifested sociopolitical uneven social order replete with glaring disparities. With palpable chemistry between the stellar cast, a non sequitur fight scene bringing the play to a bizarre yet touching crescendo, Existentialist ideologies amidst pandemic quarantined musings asking us to reexamine our purpose, conventions and priorities during our impromptu stillness, ostracized individuals feeling seen and known for who they really are only some of the major themes. There were some guttural laughs and guffaws resounding from the audience including myself brought about by the play's dark comedic genius or madness interchangeably, made even funnier and even more awkward since I was seated next to an austere male audience member who tensed up annoyingly every time I dared to enjoy myself. I once read that if you don't like something change it, if you can't change it, you can laugh at it. Well this play proffers ample opportunities for laughter and more importantly, proffers possibilities for change in the form of a brighter more equitable future. It is a miscible concoction heralding inclusivity and equity for those living seemingly in the perspicuous margins of humanity.

The staging illuminated subtle balances of light and shadow adding to the perceived nefarious undercurrent embodied within this cryptic tension filled drama. It made me think about things. I find it rather questionable how some sanctimonious humans see it fit to torment and torture "other" humans simply because they are different from them. Why not question why you may think you matter more or you matter less than your neighbor? The play argues that it is imperative that we question long established social conventions and disparate hierarchical structures of power; an ideal world would be where power is sought, power is achieved and ultimately power is shared. Is that too much to hope for in an increasingly changing world? Haven't we progressed enough as a civilization? All marginalized "others" vying for a morsel of the American Dream…perhaps it might prove more viable to "live and let live" as the dictum goes…Is the possibility for equality such a farfetched ideology?

*Witch* speaks to the empirical manifestation of worldwide protests against societal polarities. The play basically woke me up from a long quarantined aesthetical sleep and catapulted me into the world of the occult, myth, intrigue and the communal hallowed earnest yearnings of humanity striving for something better than what is immanent; compounded by a sterling cast whose astute banter and chemistry ricocheted like a ghostly yet robust echo around the stage, making for tender magnanimous moments of artistic excellence, exhortation and pure exhilaration! This play confirmed why I love the theater. I give this bewitching gem a 5 out of 5 stars!

"Gay people are all like Superman. You have to be quite strong to be gay - or to be different in any way. You build special muscles."

Noel Fielding

## Exploring the Arts: Celebrating Perpetuating and Challenging Stereotypes in the Lgbtqia Community in "Another Gay Movie"

I have yet to see a mainstream movie as explicit as "Another Gay Movie!" I recently saw this film at the Kendal Square Cinema and to say that I was blown away would be a grave understatement! This movie is like "American Pie" turned up more than just a few notches for alternative lifestyles.

The movie parodies cult classics like Stephen King's "Carrie" about an ugly duckling who was shunned at her senior prom, "Mommy Dearest" which depicts Joan Crawford and the evils of wire hangers and most daringly the gay sex, drug, and party scene with mega Gay porn star Mathew Rush!

This cinematic gem begins in a high school classroom with a male student eying the tight round muscular derriere of a male teacher, who happens to be an accented foreigner with a penchant for youngsters. The teacher then calls the student to the front of the class to answer a question on the blackboard. The student, realizing that he is hiding an erection that defiantly protrudes from his loins, tries to hide it behind a notebook. By the time he gets to the board, the notebook falls revealing his towering manhood. To his delight, he looked down to see the teacher' own pleasure wand returns the favor. Then the teacher immediately bends the student over his desk and proceeds to bang the lust out of the horny student! But wait, there is more.

It all turns out to be a daydream that the student snaps out of when the school bell rings. So begins this sex filled journey of this motley crew of jocks, nerds and misfits all trying to get laid after graduation and before the end of summer vacation.

First there is the "Jock" who all the boys look up to because he is mistakenly perceived as being very experienced and has a really big—errrr--- "squirt gun" to say the least. Second, there is the "ugly duckling" that is secretly in love with the jock but is too insecure to confess his affections for him. Third you have the "flamboyant queen of queens" who is searching for a "daddy" type to love him and whose mother is in total denial about his apparent gayness, or so he thinks. And lastly there is the loud galloping lesbian who claims that she knows more about being a man then the boys she is friends with and claims to be a sexual savant.

With an astonishingly talented cast of young actors whose chemistry together smolders the screen, this whimsical comedy takes us along on a most absorbing journey of self-discovery. It is more than just a coming of age comedy. It delves into the world of gay and lesbian identity. I find that it explored more aspects of being gay than being a lesbian. It exposed the sexual proclivities of some gay man, like an organization of men who love boys exclusively, bondage and discipline, the use of urination and defecation during sex and an array of sex toys to enhance sexual pleasures. And that's not even the half of it! You have to see it to believe it!

Some would say that the movie portrays the gay community as sex obsessed perverts. But on the other hand, similar movies like "American Pie" portrays the heterosexual youth culture in a comparable light but with less accusations of being too overtly sexual from critics. In reality, Straights are just as horny as Gays. I have yet to see the research to prove otherwise.

The movie examines more than just the burgeoning sexualities of young gay adults with a comedic twist. It successfully contends with the issue of self-acceptance, achieving love based on trust and respect and how ultimately creating a family outside of the nuclear family so to help withstand the stings of persecution for being "different" in modern society.

I literally felt like a fly on someone's wall and I got to see and hear things that I would have never heard otherwise. This movie will satisfy the curiosities of both Straights and Gays alike.

As the movie winds down, everyone got what he or she wanted in the end, so to speak. But trust me, you have to see it to believe it! No amount of words can do this campy cult classic justice. The script is so well written that it draws you into the action from start to finish, and believe you me; there is plenty of action to be drawn into.

By the end, I felt like I had just seen Shakespeare's "A Midsummer Night's Dream". A play based on an excursion of romance and sexual chaos with the wrong people falling in love. It is fitting I should offer Puck's—the vivacious fairy character in the play, final thoughts: "If these shadows have offended, think but this and all is mended, that we have but slumbered here while these visions did appear, and this weak and idle theme, no more yielding than a dream." I can't wait for the sequel!

> "A symphony must be like the world. It must contain everything"
>
> Gustav Mahler

## *Exploring the Arts: Beethoven's "Ode to Joy" Brought the House Down at Symphony Hall*

*Opening Doors to the Arts* organization provided me with complimentary tickets to ubiquitous deaf composer Ludwig Van Beethoven's Symphony No. 9 (which "traces a path from darkness to light...and the struggle for clarification..." as written by Michael Steinberg) on Friday February 24, 2023 for the 8pm showing. It is a socially relevant theme as the world struggles to navigate socio political divisions while war rages overseas and as we struggle to make sense of it all...

I was able to view the YouTube talk by conductor Benjamin Zander as well as being able to catch the pre-show talk about Beethoven's intended meaning to his iconic symphony on its 200th anniversary celebration, which Zander mentions is celebrated every ten years, and him being 80, is probably the penultimate time he will be conducting this masterpiece at Symphony Hall, the last time being the pending Carnegie Hall performance in New York City.

It was a packed crowd, even on a freezing winter evening, the audience was buzzing with anticipation creating frenetic ambient vibes, which I thought was surprising for a "classical music performance" and not a rock and roll concert. The familiarity with Beethoven's Symphony No. 9 **"Ode to Joy"** (which was a poem meant as a drinking song originally written by German poet, playwright and philosopher Freidrich Schiller who studied under another famous German poet and playwright Goethe" was succoring to the soul, it expressed you're home now probably to many of us who have heard that concerto copiously in times of jubilant celebrations like the Olympics and anytime anyone in the "winners circle" is being celebrated...Words like "crescendo", "clarinets" "bassoons" "woodwinds", "cellos", "lower strings", and "adagio", shattered the peace before bringing us back to a state of calm enjoyment. It definitely kept the audience on edge and awake! What a "joy"!

# Exploring the Arts as the Community Arts Center Offers an Alternative to Violence

The world today is maligned with concurrent tragedies permeating in and outside of the United States. With the on surge of Catastrophes like 9/11, the tsunami, Hurricane Katrina and more recently the colossal earthquake in Haiti, all leaves one to wonder: can we still be optimistic about the future? The answer is a resonant "Yes!" And I'll tell you why.

There is a place where young people congregate and it's called *The Community Arts Center* (CAC). Founded in 1932 by a group of local parents, the Community Art Center's mission is to nurture children and young adults with limited access to financial resources so they achieve personal and cultural growth, and have a positive impact on their world through joyful experiences in the arts. It can be described as the heart and soul of Cambridge's youths and "hope" has been keeping residence there for over 30 years. It is a "neighborhood institution committed to nurturing low-income children and young adults so they achieve personal and cultural growth and have a positive impact on their world through joyful experiences in the arts." It houses the Teen Media Program (TMP), which since its inception in 1970, have served over 1,000 students who have used their experience to commence careers as artists, musicians, teachers and ultimately community leaders.

The program involves youths in video productions and also provides opportunities for monetary compensation for advanced students as part of the Genuine Productions youth-managed video enterprise. The classes present a forum for analytical and productive dialogue regarding relevant issues in their lives with a configuration designed to suit individual needs. Participants may also choose to partake in the *"Do It Your Damn Self"* (DIYDS) National Youth Video and Film Festival, which is orchestrated by participants who assist in curating, hosting, promoting, as well as standardizing the event.

"The Teen Media Program challenges us to think about the world around us as well as to improve our interpersonal and technical skills," said one Teen. TMP participants generate eight to ten inventive, superior quality media ventures. Participants are expected to become versed in the importance and rationale behind artistic inventions. The program also encourages dialoguing and understanding of how media is used as a tool for social change and essentially catapulting Teens into leadership roles in their respective communities.

The program has also won numerous awards including the "Anti-Violence" award from the *Cambridge Peace Commission* and the prestigious "Coming Up Taller" award from President George W. Bush's *Committee on the Arts and the Humanities* for being one of the nation's best programs to "enable young people to nurture their interests under the disciplined and caring tutelage of educators and community leaders," wrote Leslie Brokaw of the Boston Sunday Globe. "Given the right environment, youths can do some amazing things. Film can be used as an organizational tool to understand your community. So our message is to stop complaining and do something," said Linwood Harper, TMP teacher. The center is completely funded by grants and it's free of charge to the participants. It provides local Teens from Newtowne Court and Washington Elms public housing developments in Cambridge with a safe place to cultivate and aggrandize their artistic abilities.

"Young people are attracted to this program because this is a place where they are viewed as assets—as having talent to be nurtured, a vision to offer their community, and a bright future before them. And when approached with these expectations, [the] Cambridge Arts Council's youth fulfill them," said Youth Reach Program Manager H. Mark Smith of the *Massachusetts Cultural Council*.

The DIYDS National Youth Video and Film Festival is a staple of the Cambridge Arts Center and the Teen Media Program. TMP contributors curate and host the festival, which features 20 short videos chosen among 100 submissions from around the country. Places like

Africa, Brazil, United Kingdom, and America. Some of the criteria for acceptance are integrity of message, clarity of message and meets the mission of the festival, which is to raise social consciousness.

"I am a newbie," proclaims festival coordinator Annu Ross. "I'm having fun and I hope all the kids are too. In organizing this festival, I am trying to bring in a new element and I hope that they welcome it." Youth producer and festival assistant Charnee Green, who describes herself as "the link between the Adults and the Teens," said that she's been at CAC for 10 years beginning at age of 10. She produces music videos, Public Service Announcements, movies and also writes scripts.

"I grew up here. If the center wasn't here, I wouldn't be the person I am today. Having the arts is the greatest thing they could have. Kids are in a place where they are in structured activities. In my neighborhood, kids are constantly exposed to gun violence. They shouldn't have to go through that, especially being so young."

Sandra Furey Gaither, who was born and raised in Boston and whose work has been recognized by former President Bill Clinton, and the centers first black executive director said, "I want to create a new mission to endue more art, approach things in an interdisciplinary way, to expand on what's already been accomplished...raise more money for [the arts]." She goes on to say that "...art has been cut from the schools, we are it."

The festival was a colossal success! It began with a screening of Spike Lee's *"Do The Right Thing"*, followed by a panel discussion of scholars and Teen and Adult filmmakers. The audience was also invited to participate. Lee's movie was used as a prototype to help launch the festival, which immediately followed. Like Lee's movie, the issue of social responsibility was at the core of the discussion. "The most that any artist can do is to raise questions. The most important thing is to get the audience to debate amongst themselves," said Haitian-Italian-American Emerson Film Professor Robes Pierre. And there were plenty of questions up for discussion, which kept the audience thoroughly engaged. On the issue of race, one panel member commented that "Race is a conceptual idea" and that we shouldn't let it get in the way of us getting along with one another.

The festival itself was not for the weak hearted since it dealt with a plethora of hard hitting subject matters. Contemporary themes like a young black girls struggle to accept herself in a society that validates light-skinned blacks vs. dark skinned blacks in "A Girl Like Me," which won the Best Documentary Film Award for its depth of content and narrative construction. A race study done on very young black children demonstrated that when given a choice between a white doll versus a black doll, 15 out of 20 chose the white doll. And when they were asked which was the good doll and which was the bad, they chose the black doll as the bad doll, which had the audience gasping in shock! Some of the other themes were: challenging media stereotypes, exploring ones cultural heritage, what it means to be a man, staying in school, body image issues, racial injustice in the prison system, a young woman's obsession with perfection, teen pregnancy, and finally Former President Bush as "The ultimate weapon of mass destruction," which had the audience clapping feverishly!

The rapid fire Ritalin paced festival seemingly jolted the social consciousness of all present. The question and answer session afterwards was as energetic and inquisitive as the Teens themselves. One spectator said it best: "Excellent reel and true! The creative energy of these pieces put mainstream American media to shame! I've seen the future of American Media...there is hope!" Another onlooker commented, "I am shocked at how angry these kids are..." One of the Teen producers proclaimed that he makes films because he is "...outraged about what's going on and the fact that a lot of my peers aren't paying close enough attention due to too much mechanical distractions."

As I walked out of the theater in stupor at the level of artistic splendor resonating from the souls of these amazing young people, I overheard

one astounded woman utter these words: "The world is in good hands."
And I whole-heartedly agree.

For further inquiries regarding the Community Art Center and its Teen
Media Program or to make donations please call (617) 868-7100 or visit:
www.communityartcenter.org.

"From the beginnings of literature, poets and writers have based their narratives on crossing borders, on wandering, on exile, on encounters beyond the familiar. The stranger is an archetype in epic poetry, in novels. The tension between alienation and assimilation has always been a basic theme."

Jhumpa Lahiri

## Exploring the Arts as the Annual Somerville Writers' Festival Celebrates Camaraderie Creativity and Inspiration amongst the Literary Intelligentsia

The literary world is alive and well indeed. Last Sunday, the fourth annual Somerville News Writer's Festival hosted by Jimmy Tingle and sponsored by *The Somerville News*, Grub Street Writers and Porter Square Books revisited Tingle's to wow us with the best of the best in the world of poetry and prose. The event has also been held at the ubiquitous Somerville Theatre in the past.

Timothy Gager and Doug Holder co-founded the festival and have been coordinating the festival since its inception back in 2003.

Gager said, "I hoped that this event would encourage more people to do larger events like this. I'm optimistic that it will be influential to other series."

The festival has attracted a plethora of distinguished writers such as Pulitzer Prize winners Robert Olen Butler and Franz Wright last year. And this year the feature is Nick Flynn among 11 other writers. Flynn will read from his book "Another [expletive] Night in Suck City." A critically acclaimed memoir now a movie titled *Being Flynn* starring

Robert Deniro by writer-director Paul Weitz, whose previous credits include *"About a Boy"*, *"American Pie,"* and *"In Good Company."*

The other writers reading in this event are as follows. First for the fiction category are: Steve Almond, Michael McGlone (of the Hollywood movie *The Brothers Mc Mullen* 1995), Christoper Castellani, Lisa Carver and Timothy Gager.

For the poetry category: Hugh Fox, David Levitt, Marc Wildershien, Marc Goldfinger, Joana Nealon, and Doug Holder.

The featured musical performer will be Meg Hutchinson, who won many Boston awards for her debut album "Against the Grey."

"I have worked or read with many of them in the past," Gager said.

Some of the other tasks for the festival include advertisement, and individual interviews with some of the writers for Somerville News. Speaking of advertisement, Gager has appeared on my now cancelled local TV and Internet show "Dream Weavers w/ Jacques", which showed on Thursdays at 5:30 pm on Channel 9 at Cambridge Community Television (CCTV), to promote this event. "The goal is to break even. If we don't lose money, we consider it a success," said Gager.

Gager said he is a big fan of Jimmy Tingle's. "Jimmy is a great guy, funny, personable, generous and professional." Gager also spoke very highly of the writers, he are some of his comments.

"Nick Flynn is a tremendous poet; his incredible memoir is a heart wrenching story about his father. Steve Almond is probably the most entertaining reader out there. I've never seen him lay an egg."

"Michael McGlone is also known as a famous actor known for his role in "The Brothers McMullen," he said. "He is a superb writer and has an incredible reading voice. Lisa Carver is the eclectic princess of trauma. She is a brutally honest writer." And as for Gager, Doug Holder has described him as a "junk yard dog, a self-made individual who writes simple, gritty truth."

Holder said, "The Somerville News was created to reach the community. It is also committed to sponsoring and supporting the festival. We're thinking of adding workshops and book fairs to the festival. When coordinating the festival, we approach different people from both genders and ethnicities. We hope to attract a diversity of writers like female writer Sara Hannah and Haitian writer Danielle Legros."

Spare Change News poetry editor Marc Goldfinger of whom I've had the pleasure of featuring my poetry with at Walden Pond, said, "I think it's a wonderful compliment to be included in the festival. It's great to get exposure. Most of the time writers work in solitude. So to be on stage and get an immediate response to our work helps sustain us."

Ryk McIntyre said, "I performed in the 2004 Festival, alongside other poets like Reggie Gibson. It was a wonderful experience, and of course it never looks bad to have Jimmy Tingle Off Broadway Theater on your performance resume. The best thing about the event is it shows local people that the 'literary scene' isn't synonymous with distant cities, but something close enough to touch, to encourage and--if you want--to join with. Plus I think the festival is loaded with vitamins, or something."

Gager said, "To be a good writer or poet you have to exceed everything that is required from that area of writing that you are working on. You need motif and a strong visual presentation. The story has to move, the characters have to be interesting. You have to be a craftsman, the words have to sing at times and hit hard at others. Every word, every line is important in poetry. The shorter the work, the more that statement is true."

The event was a funky fusion of distinguished and accomplished writers and poets who came together to help remedy the disease of isolation and foster a sense of community collaboration and artistic integration. Songstress Meg Hutchinson provided the eager crowd with a delicious blend of Jazzy-folk tunes to help soothe the rapid fire Ritalin paced evening. She admitted to being a closet poet and that she is on the brink of coming out to share her stuff.

Tingle did a rousing rendition of humorous story telling that helped warm up the crowd before the features took the stage. He referred to Davis square as "The Paris of the West" and the theater is so hidden in its present basement location that terrorists won't be able to find him, and even if they did "where are they gonna park" he said.

Levitt gave a funny, witty and relaxed performance. The performers were all conscious of the time constraints and Doug Holder as the time police. They made fun of Holder by acting overly conscientious of time limitations, which went over well with the crowd. One audience member commented that the festival should have less people and more time for the readers.

McGlone, known for his roles in "The Brothers McMullen", "She's The One" and "Bad City" was a deep voiced thunder of artistic elegance and possessed and amazing singing voice that resonated in the cozy theater. "A magnificent gathering of authors that I thoroughly enjoyed," said McGlone as he exited the theater.

Goldfinger's reading was gripping as he expressed his dissatisfaction with the way things are in America and to galvanize us to action! He denounced the war in Iraq and passionately expressed a need for justice and equality among humanity. "We spend more money to kill than to heal," he said.

Carver chose not to read and surprised the audience by playing a DVD called "Simple Assaults" and her pirate theme left everyone flabbergasted.

And last but not least Nick Flynn, who joked that about calling a poetry book a memoir because it will sell better, invited us into his world by reading from his highly praised memoir "Another [expletive] Night in Suck City," which the audience seem to thoroughly enjoyed.

All in all, the night was a success. It did what it was meant to do: bring people together to celebrate the arts and simultaneously help foster a sense of community. The festival also offered creative inspiration and renewal to all who were willing to partake in this most prolific endeavor.

"The greatness of a community is most accurately measured
by the compassionate actions of its members."
--Coretta Scott King

# PART IV

# Community

# At Topsfield Fair, The Flying Wallendas Use Tightrope Walking To Teach Life Lessons and an Eye Opening Fact about Bees

It was a clear crisp sunny day when we boarded the bus to the Topsfield Fair, described as America's oldest fair and founded in 1818.

The bus ride itself was swift and scenic with plenty of natural esthetics to keep the visual senses in awe of environmental beauty: leafy colors of the fall, and plenty of vast farm lands and farm workers keeping America fed.

There was a bevy of scheduled activities when we arrived shortly after 11 a.m. The first thing I did when I first began to meander around was take a special effects photo on a surfboard, riding blue waves to oblivion. Then around 2 p.m. I stumbled onto the circus act: **The Flying Wallendas**, famous for their high wire daredevil performances. The Wallendas trace their intrepid roots back to 1780 Austria-Hungary. Their ancestors toured as a band of acrobats, aerialists, jugglers, animal trainers and trapeze artists. John Ringling of the Ringling Bros. and Barnum & Bailey Circus recruited the Wallendas after sighting them perform in Cuba. They got the nickname "the flying Wallendas" in the 1940s after a fall during an Akron, Ohio performance. A reporter who saw it said, the Wallendas fell so elegantly that it appeared as if they were flying. No one was wounded in that incident. I was able to get an autographed photo from the patriarch at the end of the show. He also got philosophical when he spoke about how he manages to balance and not fall when he's up there on the high wire. He said that he just identifies a point of "focus" and remains there until he crosses over safely. He said that is a method that we can all apply in other areas of our lives. As someone who is challenged by the ability to concentrate myself, I often meditate to help with focus. And now, like the flying Wallendas, I will pick a point of focus, whether that be a conjured up halcyon image in the form of my own esoteric happy place.

Some of the other activities and displays listed on the fair program during our Saturday October 8th, 2022 visit were the Bee Keeping Building where there was honey for sale, you can make your own honeycomb candles to take home with you and I learned some distinctive facts about honeybees. Did you know that honey bees fertilize about 80% of our fruits and vegetables? Or that they have five eyes and NEVER sleep?!

There was also a Youth Cattle Show and plenty of ruminants like cattle, goats and sheep, and where I saw plenty of our bovine friends lying leisurely around while being gawked at and photographed by fair onlookers. There was even a cow replica where one can use a bucket and squeeze the simulated udders for "milk" and take pictures while doing it for a fun memory. Did you know that cows can detect a scent from about 5 miles away? And that they produce about 8 gallons of milk per day? That's enough for 128 people to have a glass of milk every day! A dairy farmer will typically get paid 75% of what it costs to produce the milk. For example, a gallon of milk that costs you 3 dollars will cost 2 dollars to make, but the farmer will only get paid $1.50.

There were also New England Equine (horse) Rescue shows, dairy goat shows, cock crowing and hen flying contests, swine racing and swimming pigs! There was a hot dog eating contest happening around 3 p.m. concurrently while we were readying to board the bus back to Boston. There were a few mishaps, some people got lost, including myself, but were eventually found. It was a great opportunity for relatable camaraderie with others without the annoying distraction of technology. To my surprise, NO one had their heads down scanning their phones. It's a step towards individual and community connection in a world of increasing disconnection from ourselves and our communities. I hope to "find myself" there again next year!

"A neoliberal disaster is one who generates a mass incarceration regime, who deregulates banks and markets, who promotes chaos of regime change in Libya, supports military coups in Honduras, undermines some of the magnificent efforts in Haiti of working people, and so forth."

Cornel West

# Exploring Unity in Community at The Annual Urban Walk for Haiti

Martin Luther King Jr. once said "Life's most urgent question is: what are you doing for somebody else?" So let's take a moment to remember the less fortunate than us instead of accumulating more "stuff" that we don't really need. We must take advantage of opportunities to land a hand to help pull Third World countries like Haiti out of misery and such opportunity has arrived in the form of The 8th Annual Urban Walk for Haiti! The walk will be sponsored by *Partners In Health (PIH)*, a Boston based charity organization spearheaded by noted Harvard University Professor and anthropologist Dr. Paul Farmer, that help provide education and health care to the people of Haiti. Its vision is both medical and moral; grounded on both solidarity as well as charity. PIH was founded in 1987, two years after the Clinique Bon Sauveur was set up in Cange, Haiti, to deliver health care to the residents of the mountainous Central Plateau. PIH co-founders had been working in the area for years. The Clinic was just the first of an arc of successful projects designed to address the health care needs of the residents of the poorest area in Haiti. In the 20 years since then, PIH has expanded its operations to eight other sites in Haiti and five additional countries.The walk proceeds are disseminated to the construction and maintenance of schools, hospitals and shelter. It will also help supply medicine, improve water and food programs and elevate the standard of living for Haitians.

"Dr. Farmer is known for his support of a Preferential Option for the Poor, a central Tenet of Liberation Theology" according to Walk for Haiti General Outreach Coordinator Karen Fritsche. She goes on to say that, "His approach to practice in Haiti, Peru and Russia has its basis in ethnographic analysis and real world practicality. Mountains Beyond Mountains: The Quest of Dr. Paul Farmer, a Man Who Could Cure the World by Tracy Kidder details Farmer's work in Haiti and abroad…" The ubiquitous Dr. Paul Farmer is an avid supporter of Haiti and he wears many hats; he is a Harvard University professor; a practicing physician; author and founder of Partners in Health (PIH). Partners in Health is a Boston based organization that supports in part Dr. Farmer's hospitals in Haiti, which are free to all patients.

Ms. Fritsche, a former French teacher at Lincoln-Sudbury Regional High School, related the story of how the walk for Haiti begun involving one of her former students. Gerald Mc. Elroy, then a 10th grader, told Ms. Fritsche that he wanted to help Dr. Farmer. Gerald suggested to Ms. Fritsche that the French Club should launch a walk to raise money and help support the philanthropic initiatives of Dr. Farmer. She said she thought it was a good idea and wanted to give it some thought, but Gerald said abruptly "You have to do it!" She asked why? To which he responded "I've already charged $400 dollars on my father's credit card on T-Shirts for the walkers, aren't they lovely? I designed them myself." According to Ms. Fritsche, her reaction was both exhilaration and apprehension of what young Gerald's actions implied.

So began the Annual Urban Walk for Haiti, which has been going on for the past eight years. It is a community event aimed at raising money and awareness for the western hemisphere's once richest island in the Americas when Christopher Columbus arrived on the land he called 'Hispaniola' or 'Little Spain' on Dec. 5, 1492. Gerald today still remains vehemently involved with the walk on a variety of levels, including constructing and maintaining the website www.walkforhaiti.org. Ms. Fritsche emphasized that absolutely 100% percent of the proceeds from the walk would go to the projects that are housed by Partners in Health in the Central Plateau, which is North East of Port-au-Prince, one of Haiti's poorest areas. "If we can't see God in the poorest of the poor, we will never find him," says Fritsche.

According to Andrew Marx, manager of Communications for PIH, the health care system in the Central Plateau, which has a total of seven hospitals, is said to be so superior that they have a waiting list of patients from the capital Port-au-Prince and Miami! "They even have 'Accompagnateurs' or Social Workers" says Marx. "Their roles are to make sure that their neighbors have access to help when they need it, a sort of outreach to provide health education, Directly Observed Therapy to insure that they take their medications, have enough to eat and monitor their general living conditions." He also added that those "Social Workers" are often illiterate but are provided with the proper training.

PHI also provides aid to Guatemala, Peru, Mexico, Russia, Rwanda hospitals and feeding programs. The Clinton Foundation was looking for a successful program to fight Aids and drug-resistant Tuberculosis in poor countries. PHI is the model utilized by the World Health Organization in the fight against Aids and multi-drug resistant Tuberculosis. Ms. Fritsche is aware that some may say that PIH by definition should be geared towards just health care but she also emphasizes that education and food are both necessary to be considered healthy. "In Haiti, kids are dying as young as 20-years-old because they have no way to make a living. They succumb to malnutrition, aids and prostitution." She goes on to say that, "…the emphasis is on raising funds for education, especially for a secondary, international baccalaureate school, run by PIH, and, if funds are left over, to begin construction of a university on the Cange socio-medical complex of PIH. We are meeting Dr. Farmer's request for funds to return children to a normal life post-quake, both children in the Cange region that were not destroyed by the quake, and children streaming in from Port-au-Prince and the surrounding area who are traumatized by the quake, some of whom are orphaned and/or injured, all of whom are suffering from trauma and shock." PIH focuses on a community-based model, where they train local Doctors and health workers. When a person falls ill, PIH uses all of the means at

[its] disposal to make them well—from pressuring drug manufacturers, to lobbying policy makers, to providing medical care and social services. Whatever it takes. Just as we would do if a member of our own family— or we ourselves—was ill." (Source: www.PIH.org)

This event has gone beyond the involvement of the French club to a broader spectrum of eager participants including Harvard, Yale, MIT, Boston University, 15 high schools and fifteen church groups from a multitude of cities including by not limited to Somerville, Cambridge and the Greater Boston area. "In past years, over 1000 have marched and this year we're expecting even more people to join us!" said Ms. Fristche.

In response to the tragedy on January 12, the Walk for Haiti committee has developed a three-part approach to this year's event: (1) awareness, (2) recovery and (3) hope. We aim to educate people about Haiti, its rich history, culture and resilient spirit; to focus a significant amount of attention and energy on helping Haiti recover through the fundraising effort itself; and to use the funds raised on the day of the walk to facilitate the construction of schools to accommodate refugee children, who are streaming into the Central Plateau from Port-au-Prince. 100% of all funds raised directly support this effort. The Walk has helped equip operating rooms, provide community health education and schooling (including scholarships for over 800 students).

Last year, the urban walk for Haiti raised $71,000 dollars. PIH was able to use 100% of the funds to provide education to 203 high school students, all of whom passed the baccalaureate. The money raised paid for school fees, uniforms, books, one meal a day and augmented teachers' salaries at an annual cost of $350 dollars per student. In the eight years since a small group of students and teachers came together to bring relief to a struggling Haitian people, a total of more than $325, 000 dollars has been raised..After last year's devastating earthquake, Haiti has again been hard hit by tragedy with its first epidemic of cholera in over 40 years. This year's funds will directly support the Partners In Health's 'Zanmi Agrikol (Creole for 'friend of agriculture') project- a critical effort to combat pediatric malnutrition by locally producing and then distributing two therapeutic ready to use food supplements called Nourimil and Nourimanba. It currently costs $150 dollars to nourish a child for 6 to 8 weeks with special programs using food supplements to recover a child from severe malnutrition. $3.06 per day to save a child! (Source www.walkforhaiti.org).

The walk is a cultural experience consisting of a Haitian market place, and entertainment which will feature an all-female Haitian music ensemble ZiliMisik, along with Haitian drumming, a Haitian choir, dance, food, crafts and a few speakers. Pledge sheets are on the walk website, which also has flyers and instructions to group leaders that can be downloaded. Donations of $100 dollars or more gets you a commemorative T-Shirt. Individuals are invited to bear witness to greatness in local communities. Come celebrate at the pre-walk party and familiarize yourself with an unfamiliar country.

For more information visit the website: www.walkforhaiti.org.

# Celebrating Community as the First Baptist Church Deemed Historical Landmark Celebrates 190 Years of Service to the Cambridge Neighborhood And Where Dr. Martin Luther King Jr. Once Spoke

In a world where mainstream media constantly offers us things to carp about, today I'm here to tell you something to rejoice about: **The 190th Anniversary "Signs of Life" Celebration at the Historic First Baptist Church** in Central Square Cambridge, Massachusetts where Martin Luther King Jr. once preached. It is written that "the history of the First Baptist Church consists of an invisible fabric of Christian mettle, fired by the spirit of God, who inspired those who have gone before and those who currently fellowship together to take the message of the gospel into the world."

The primary movers of this ambitious project are Pastor John Harry Petter and Church member and entrepreneur Lynette Laveau Saxe. They both claim that the Church attracts people from all over the world including Scotland, Tennessee, North Carolina, Liberia, Kenya and Nova Scotia. However, they are aware that certain populations like young people and young families are missing. The median age of attendees is 60.

Pastor Petter originated the concept "Signs of Life" because of the lack of activity surrounding the Church and is clearly manifested by the Cambridge community. The one thing that is constantly visible and in essence produce any "signs of life" are the 12 Step groups that meet in the Church. Pastor Petter affirms that the Church is open to provide the community with an opportunity to interact with the congregation. He also states that the self- help groups like Alcoholics Anonymous, Narcotics Anonymous, Gamblers Anonymous, Anger Management,

Work-a-holics Anonymous are subsidized by the Church and thus are part of the Church.

Laveau who staged the play *"Moments of Courage in American History: The Underground Railroad"* back a few years ago in this particular Church stated that it was a stop along the underground railroad and has been designated a landmark since it is over a hundred years old. Petter proposes that the community come and be part of a renewed faith and that the purpose of Church is spiritual not material; which explains why the Church is not charging admission but simply asking for a donation to attend the upcoming events.

Petter wants you to participate in the process of understanding of what it means to be a Christian. He uses the following metaphor to illustrate what he perceives as the way to construct the Church community. He says it's like building a vehicle together. One person brings a fender, another steering wheel, another door, another radiator until the vehicle is complete and runs smoothly as one entity. Laveau explained that if one part is broken, by the end you will find that all the parts have been renewed if we all make a contribution. This brings to mind the popular saying "No man is an island" which was originated by the philosopher John Dunne. And Laveau affirms this by stating that "No one succeeds alone."

Petter wants to eradicate the outer image of inactivity that hovers like a cloud over the Church and replace it with a flowing spring of growth and activism. He also claims that contemporary liturgy is predicated by the growth factor. He says that the celebration is looking backwards in order to go forward and Laveau asserts that it's intended to make the Church more interactive with the community. The Church is located at 5 Magazine Street, Cambridge, MA.

"According to [Charles] Darwin's *Origin of Species*, it is not
the most intellectual of the species that survives; it is not the
strongest... but the species that... that is able... to adapt and
adjust to the changing environment in which it finds itself.
--Leon C. Megginson,
Louisiana State University Professor
In his interpretation of the central
Idea outlined in Darwin's
"*On the Origin of Species*"
At the 1963 convention of
Southwestern Social Science Association

# PART V

# *Resiliency*

# Exploring the Buoyant Spirit of Haiti in the Beijing Olympics

The American media, for the most part, do not portray Haiti in a positive light. America's relationship with Haiti is tense to say the least. Maybe it's because Haiti is the first Black Republic, achieving independence from slavery and French occupation in the 19th Century under the brave leadership of Jean-Jacques Dessaline and Toussaint Louverture. American philanthropist Dr. Paul Farmer of Harvard University, who does miraculous work in third world countries like Haiti, have even written a book about how America have exploited and depleted Haiti's resources aptly titled "The Uses of Haiti." However America often pontificate that Haiti is an extremely poor country; which is to me equivalent to pulling someone's eyes out and then accusing them of being blind.

Inspite of all the country's been through and is currently going through, their resilience is being portrayed in the 2008 Olympic Games in Beijing, China where there is only a hand full of Haitian Athletes. The Haitian delegation to the Beijing Olympics consists of 5 members most notably Nadine Faustin-Parker, whose been adorned with the axiom "rising star." It has been emphasized that Haiti's probability of winning gold in Beijing is enormously scant, but the Haitian deputation is quite pleased to personify their homeland.

The five-member delegation will compete in diverse areas such as boxing, taekwondo and track, which will essentially feature Haiti's rising track star Nadine-Faustin-Parker. Unfortunately, Haiti has not won a medal in the Olympics since 1928, when Silvio Cator achieved a silver medal in the men's long jump. Parker is painfully aware that her chances of ending that dearth are faint, but hopefully she will rise up to the challenge and make history yet again. Her aspiration is to transcend her performance in Athens and make the final of the 100-metre hurdles.

However, she has covert reasons for desiring to excel at the Olympic Games.

Faustin-Parker was born in Brussels in 1976 to Haitian parents and lived for the most part in New York. Running was always a big part of her life, but when the time came to choose which country to represent, she never had much doubt. "My parents have always kept me close to my Haitian roots, so I never felt just because I was outside the country that I wasn't part of it," she explicated. Faustin-Parker has already achieved the coveted title of being Haiti's most successful ever-female track athlete. "Competing for Haiti gave me a purpose," she said. "I enjoy the challenge of trying to put a country on the map. Some Haitian youths are ashamed of their roots, and that's something I never was so I try to make them understand they have a lot to be happy about."

Faustin-Parker's very first Olympic Games were in 2000, when injury constrained her to the quarter-finals, and even though she ran her personal best four years later it was not sufficient to make the final. Now, however, she is assured that her time to shine under the Beijing sun has come. "I would not be competing right now if I didn't believe it," says Faustin-Parker. In accordance with her website, the "NAD" in Nadine represents *Never Accept Defeat*. Faustin-Parker, who works part-time at the University of North Carolina as Director of Track and Field competitions, aspires to become Haiti's Sports Ambassador. "The better I perform at the Games, the easier it will be to make contacts and gain sponsors," she explicated. "I really want to build a track in Haiti. I see what track and field has done all over the world for the youth. It can really help somebody move forward in life."

Too often the Haitian community does not support one another in the pursuit of greatness so that they can make a mark in their respective communities. Take Haitian restaurants for example, Somerville's *Sunrise Cuisine* and *Highland Cuisine* in particular. Restaurant owners tend to be content just to cater to their own people. They only advertise on Haitian radio, Haitian television and Haitian newspapers, rather than expose their business to mainstream media as well to help fortify and aggrandize their business and presence in this country. I have extended offers to Haitian businesses to possibly feature them in some of the newspapers I write for at no cost to them and they have ignored my generosity of spirit. We need more collaboration in the Haitian community. Another example of the Haitian community's isolation from non- Haitians is The Annual Urban Walk for Haiti, which is a committee of people like myself, who gather to raise money for *Partners in Health*, an organization spearheaded by Dr. Paul Farmer of Harvard University that builds schools and hospitals in Haiti free to the public. I find myself burdened with melancholy to see that most of the people at the walk for Haiti are *not* Haitians. One person said it best from the website "HaitiXchange," which is a forum for verbal expression: "One problem I have always had with bringing anything dealing with putting efforts towards progress with us Haitian people...we never seem to think that our pessimistic views are what is killing us...we always look at why should we then why not." Well Nadine Faustin-Parker is looking at "Why not" in China and so should we in America.

"I think Haiti is a place that suffers so much from neglect that people only want to hear about it when it's at its extreme. And that's what they end up knowing about it."

Edwidge Danticat

# Haiti Also Rises: The History of Haiti's Resiliency against International Cruelty

"'History is the memory of states', wrote Henry Kissinger in his book *A World Restored* in which he proceeded to tell the history of 19th century Europe from the point of view of the leaders of Austria and England, ignoring the millions who suffered from those state men's policies."

The aforementioned is from Howard Zinn's revolutionary book: *A People's History of the United States*. It depicts U.S. history from the point of view of the common man. His method of operation is in direct correlation to what I'm about to do: tell you Haiti's history from my point of view. History is not necessarily or essentially "the memory of states" as Kissinger puts it. It is the narrative of the people whose lives were impacted, fragmented or altogether destroyed by intransigent politics and capricious foreign policies of dominant powers.

First and foremost, I want to outline Haiti's historical chronology; thus giving you a theoretical basis from which you can begin to undergo a more comprehensive understanding of the country's history and its present state of political and environmental instability.

In 1492, Christopher Columbus landed on the island and named it Hispaniola. Taino-Arawak Indians, who referred to their homeland as "Hayti" or "Mountainous Land", originally inhabited the island. In 1697 slaves were sent to Haiti. The island was cherished by European powers for its natural resources, including cocoa, cotton and sugar cane. And so the French shipped in thousands of slaves mainly from West Africa to harvest the crops. In 1804 after a slave rebellion led by a man named Boukman in 1791, Haiti became the first black independent state under General Jean-Jacques Dessalines, who declared himself Emperor. America feared that the slave rebellion in Haiti would ignite anti-slavery insurgents in the southern U.S. states. Perhaps this is one of the reasons America's relationship with Haiti is strained to this day. In 1844, after decades of strife and multiple rulers, the island was split into two nations: Haiti and the Dominican Republic.

In 1915, U.S. marines occupied Haiti to [supposedly] calm a state of anarchy. The Americans improved the infrastructure while helping to create the Haitian armed forces. In 1957 a reign of terror began when Francois "Papa Doc" Duvalier seizes power. His son, Jean-Claude "Baby Doc" Duvalier then just 18 years old, took over in 1971, continuing his father's legacy of tyranny. In 1986, a rebellion ignited. As protests gathered steam, the U.S. arranged exile in France for Baby Doc and his family. In 1990, after decades of dictatorship, former Roman Catholic Priest Jean-Bernard Aristide, becomes Haiti's first freely elected leader. In 1991, after a military incursion, Aristide is ousted and is forced to seek exile in the U.S. The coup ignited a mass exodus with more than 40, 000 Haitians rescued by the U.S. coast guard during a twelve-month period. In 1996 Rene Preval becomes president.

In 2000 Aristide is elected once again. In 2004 political violence plagues the Haitian capital, with accusations of a fraudulent election looming, a few weeks after Haiti celebrates in 200th anniversary, a rebel movement usurps control and Aristide is forced into exile again. Deadly floods leave 2,000 dead and causing deforestation. In 2006 Preval is elected in the first election since Aristide was overthrown in 2004. In 2008 food prices in Haiti aggrandized as they have elsewhere in the world but the situation on the island was exacerbated since most Haitians only live on $2.00 dollars per day. Also deadly hurricanes left 23, 000 homes destroyed, many dead and 70 percent of the nation's crops wiped out. In 2010, an earthquake with a magnitude of 7.0 ambushed

Port-au-Prince, collapsing buildings with 100,000 thousand estimated dead. World Vision—an organization that has worked in Haiti for thirty years—makes an expedited trip to the island rushing emergency supplies to the survivors.

A great man once said, "Life's most important question is: What are you doing for somebody else?" Dr. Paul Farmer, a Harvard Professor and anthropologist, is an avid supporter of Haiti. He became involved with the country when he went on a school trip as an undergraduate student. Today, he has spearheaded the ubiquitous Boston based organization *Partners in Health (P.I.H)*, devoted to aiding third world countries like Haiti. Farmer is known for his support of a Preferential Option for the Poor, a central precept of Liberation Theology. His approach to practice in Haiti, Peru and Russia has its basis in ethnographic analysis—the science that studies and compares human cultures—and real world practicality. Mountains Beyond Mountains: The Quest of Dr. Paul Farmer, A Man Who Could Cure the World by Tracy Kidder details Farmer's work in Haiti and abroad. I have been a part of P.I.H. since I was bestowed with the honor of being the Official Poet and Publicity Coordinator for the Annual Urban Walk for Haiti, which raises monies for P.I.H.

In Haiti, it was common knowledge that one's own friends could be bribed as spies and government informants. Their jobs were to safeguard the brutal reigning regime by turning in anyone whom they considered subversive. Under the Haitian weather, the wind in the trees often swirled about all the fetid feeling of death and despair. However, contrary to what the American news media has imprinted as fact in the heads of people across the world, Haiti has more dimensions than the poor, the poorer and the poorest.

There are three classes of people: the bourgeoisie, the middle class and then the poor. I was part of the middle class. Both my parents owned property in Port-au-Prince and my father was a clothes designer, retail storeowner and mercantile entrepreneur. He was also a land and multiple homeowner, which he rented as part of his entrepreneurial endeavors.

My mother was a house wife, socialite and landlord with a degrees in cosmetology and the culinary arts. I attended an exclusive private school near the Haitian palace called Frere Andre (Brother Andre). It was there that I leaned how *not* to think for myself through blatant memorization of pedantic texts and taking dictations to prepare me for the dictatorship of the ruling class. Today, however, my childhood home is a trumpeting pile of dilapidated earthquake muddy putty. My families are all alive but some are displaced and expectedly traumatized, as am I. But Haiti is more than just doom and gloom.

I remember staring in stupor the dance of the Caribbean wind over the azure sea, the deep green elegance of the palms, picnic by moonlight and sweet memories of mangoes. Purple butterflies, a visual feast of dancing loveliness, under the flowery spring sun. The joyous sounds of laughter resounding from the young as they run about playing hide and seek during blackouts. But unfortunately, there also lied in the sea a maelstrom of fear, violence, misery and poverty, which most can barely swim out of, while the orchestrating powers that ensnare them stand by cross armed and snarling. But one day, it is my fervent hope that Haitian children will wake up to shiny silver mornings and hummingbirds singing, promising freedom, serenity and prosperity.

We lived in a world dominated by the hetero sexist macho male culture. However, my mother Marie-Evelyne Toussaint, who bears the same name as Haitian rebel fighter Toussaint L'ouverture, was and still is iconoclastic in that she dared to be a leader for her family when most women were subjected to being simply subservient to the men. Since we were considered middle class, she became caught up in the gaudy accoutrements of upward mobility, so when the Haiti's political and economic crises began to converge, threatening our lifestyle, we all came to America. She related to me that under the Duvalier dictatorship, tourism in Haiti flourished from the 1950's all the way up to 1986, practically ending with the Baby Doc mutiny. Foreign groups like Arabs, Lebanese, and even Chinese exiled from their respective countries lived and built businesses in Haiti. Also Haiti's number one tourist attraction, *La Citadelle Laferriere,* built on mountains overlooking Port-au-Prince

17 miles south of the city of Cap Haitien by Henry Christopher—a general in the Haitian army—has walls 130 feet high is the largest fortress in the Americas and was designated by the United Nations Educational, Scientific and Cultural Organization (UNESCO) as a world history site in 1982. It was built to keep the newly independent nation from French incursions, which never materialized.

Haitians in American are for the most part hard working honest and joyous intelligent people. Most of the women work as Certified Nursing Assistants in Nursing Home facilities, caring for America's elderly population and a plethora of men work as cab drivers. Large majorities also attend college to become doctors, lawyers, engineers and nurses. Both the men and women pursue the American Dream by buying cars and houses, sometimes working two to three jobs. I too am living my version of the American dream by graduating from college with honors (Phi Beta Kappa) and publishing my first autobiography of prose and poetry aptly titled *Sparks in the Dark*, which was featured in the Boston Globe. Yet still, there seems to be an undercurrent of fear and hatred towards the Haitian population here in the States. Maybe it's because the conscientious and resultant collaboration of the "Have Nots" that often instigate the principal fears and resistance of the "Haves", since the rich want to remain rich and in control. Robert Lawless, quoted in Farmer's book *The Uses,* asserts "Haitians are the immigrants Americans love to fear and hate." But why, I ask of you? Which leads me to ponder, is hate and prejudice ever truly justified?

"Why should we care about Haiti?" writes politico and M.I.T professor Noam Chomsky in the introduction to Farmer's book *The Uses.* "...we are the richest and most powerful country in the world, while Haiti is at the opposite extreme of human existence: miserable, horrifying, black, ugly. We may pity Haitians and other backwards people who have, unaccountably, failed to achieve our nobility and wealth, and we may even try to lend a hand, out of humanitarian impulse. But responsibility stops there." I once heard the adage "If your neighbors house is on fire, wet yours." As we know tragedy affects all of us, having experienced hurricane Katrina, and 9/11. In relation to American occupation of

Haiti, Chomsky goes on to say, "In a situation of domination and occupation, the occupier... has to justify what it's doing. There is only once way to do it—become a racist. You have to blame the victim. Once you've become a raving racist in self-defense, you've lost your capacity to understand what's [really] happening." In other words, it's like putting someone's eyes out and then accusing them of being blind. America's exploitation of Haiti, it's support of the Duvaliers and the military for the repression of the Haitian people and expedient U.S. foreign policies and an ongoing debate about Haitian asylum seekers, are all impediments to the progression of the Haitian nation. It seems like light skinned immigrants like Cubans and Mexicans get asylum, why not Haitians?

"How far you go in life depends on your being tender with the young, compassionate with the aged, sympathetic with the striving and tolerant of the weak and strong. Because someday in your life you will have been all of these."

George Washington Carver

## *Dancing with Demons: A Mental Health Malady Survivor Story*

One restless night among the many restless nights of living a life marred with relentless anxiety and depression, He dreamt that he was walking along a boardwalk somewhere in America with his psychiatrist walking alongside him, trying desperately to talk him out of ending his life. He said, "You are not the only one who feels lonely. You are not the only one who feels isolated. You are not the only one who feels abandoned. You are not the only one who feels empty, devoid of any energy or desire to get up in the morning, devoid of any motivation to do anything except wait for death to knock at your door; when you'll gladly answer it out of pure desperation to escape the persistent pain of living with this depression monster that is slowly killing you inside." And just when he thought that the dream couldn't get any weirder, Cher came strutting down the board walk in that notorious fishnet outfit she wore in the video "If I Could Turn Back Time"; she took his hand and they began to slow dance to her song: "We All Sleep Alone." And then of course he reluctantly woke up!

He has had depression as far as he could remember; that would be as far back as the age of 10 when he was still in birth country, before he came to America at an early age. He remembers feeling very alone, even as he played with all his cousins and neighborhood kids. One time, he remembered stepping out of the house and all the kids playing outside yelled "His out! His out!" and he rushed right back into his own self-imposed isolation and that was when his private hell began. But as often is the case with any type of mental illness, there is usually a genetic predisposition combined with environmental infractions that often triggers the disease; having endured psychological and physical abuse from a violent alcoholic family member for nearly two decades was certainly one of the catalysts that triggered his depression. Later on in life, he learned from his mother that he had an uncle (his father's brother) who was mentally ill as well. His mother told him that his father was ashamed of his brother. His uncle ended up committing suicide by stepping in front of an oncoming train.

Then he learned that he also had a brother from his father's side who, like him, was a tortured soul and he too ended up committing suicide. He can only speculate at this point when trying to find the correlations between the psychopathology in his family and himself. However, when it comes to his own battle with mental illness, the veil of mystery attributed to his family has been lifted. He knows how he got to this point in his life, particularly now that he is experiencing a moment of psychological and spiritual health and clarity.

When he's in a depressive state, *everything* seems to require too much energy and when that happens the only thing left to do is sleep, sleep and sleep some more. He figures that is the only way to escape that contentious and continuous feeling that resides in the core of his soul; this gaping maw of emptiness and despair. And when he is finally awake, he feels so uncomfortable in his own skin that absolutely nothing he does feels satisfactory; including watching Television, reading, sitting, standing, walking, even breathing. The feeling of hopelessness is so potent that he would begin to think that death would be a welcomed alternative; since in reality, while in a state of deep depression, he feels like he is living a death in life; so the thought of being actually dead does not scare him one bit. The only thing that makes him feel better during those intense periods of depression is eating, eating and eating some more at all times of the day, particularly after midnight. Then, comes the inevitable weight gain which ends up making him feel even *more* depressed. Then comes the psychological pathology that causes him to feel irritability, anger, hostility, indifference, impervious to everyone and everything around him, ultra-sensitive, paranoid and completely delusional.

At the onset of a depressive state, the first thing he does is isolate from *everyone* including his own family. The second thing he does is start to drudge up things from the past that has happened to him or things that people have said or done to him that ended up hurting him in some way; that way he can have a prima facie rational reason to be angry and eventually lash out by making surprise verbal attacks on family and friends who try desperately to reach out to him. Soon after that, he starts to feel like he doesn't care what happens to him and/or everyone in his life and the world basically. He begins to feel emotionally and physically detached both from his inner and outer world. After that, he begins to experience the unfathomable pain of existence; a pain so intense it penetrates and permeates the very nucleus of his being; essentially causing him to ponder about an alternative in the form of *actual* physical suffering since the emotional pain gets to be too much to bare. During those times, he cries randomly about anything from his past or present. He finds himself balling his eyes out watching reality Television shows. At other times, He finds himelf crying in his sleep and waking up and still be crying even harder. When he finally manages to find some energy to leave the apartment, once outside, he starts to feel that people are staring at him or talking about him or laughing at him and paranoia eventually seizes his very soul; which forces him to go back home and continue to avoid being among the living.

Eventually, his depression eases up and he starts to come alive again and then *everything* feels like he's experiencing them for the first time; the air smells better, the sun shines brighter and his lust and love for life and the people in it seems stronger. He starts to reach out to his family, friends and the community at large. He realizes that he needs to observe these methods *during* deep periods of depression and not *after* but that's easier said than done. His psychiatrist have taken him off most of his medications upon realizing that they were making him worst and not better. Anti-depressant medications like Prozac ended up causing him to have violent tendencies; which is a total contradiction to his pacifist propensity. Now, the only medication he's on is one that helps him to sleep at night, since his mind tends to be overactive during late night hours.

Another alternative that his iconoclastic doctor suggested is a treatment plan that focuses more on a behavioral approach than the traditional medicinal one. He has recommended that he enrolls in a one to two year program called *Dialectical Behavior Therapy* (D.B.T). This program helps people with mental illness cope with everyday life by focusing on more effective ways to react to the world around them; it teaches *them* about how to be assertive without being aggressive; how to *solve* problems instead of *creating* them; how to uncover the source of their problematic behavior and ameliorate them instead of simply overreacting *because* of them and generally how to be healthier happier. He has dropped in and out of this program because it requires a tremendous amount of discipline, tenacity and readiness to complete.

The other method his doctor suggests that he tries to keep his depression from completely invading his body and spirit is to maintain a relative level of structured daily activity. He knows now that he has depression but depression doesn't have him. Mental illness can be hazardous to your health; you can't do it alone no matter what your dark mind tells you. When you feel like you're drowning, reach out and someone is bound to pull you back into the world of the living.

# Hope-in-Haiku

Our A-me-ri-ca
All colors under the same sun
Rainbow after the rain...

"We must bring the issue of mental illness out into the sunlight, out of the shadow, out of the closet, deal with it, treat people, have centers where people can get the necessary help."

John Lewis

# "I Hear Something You Can't Hear" Exploring the Subjective Experience of Mental Illness and Resiliency in "The Quiet Room": A Book Review

Imagine a world where darkness swallows darkness and swallows more darkness. Picture a world of shadows and obscurity where dogs look like wolves and a world seemingly crumbling around you waiting to be rebuilt. The world of which I speak is that of Lori Schiller's in her ghastly and chilling book "THE QUIET ROOM: A JOURNEY OUT OF THE TORMENTS OF MADNESS." The book details Lori's gruesome tale of the illness experience of the disease of schizophrenia. The illness experience differs from the disease in that it focuses more on the day-to-day effects of the disease, how it permeates over all aspects of one's life. By this I mean how it can affect family relationships, friendships, career and general interaction with the inner and outer world. In the following article, I will focus on Lori's resiliency and using aspects of the analogous theories of Carl Rogers, Alfred Adler and Carl Jung and existential ideologies to illustrate the point that in the midst of immense strife, how an individual manage to strive for purpose and meaning in their lives.

At the beginning of the book, Lori wrote *"I hear something you can't hear..."* She went on to write about how in the brevity before the darkness, how bright and beautiful the world seemed. She explained that during her seventieth year at summer camp, how "The Lake seemed more blue...the trees of the Catskill Mountains that tinged our camp took on a deeper green than I remembered...."

She goes on to say that she was "...overwhelmed by what life had to offer." And that she "could not run fast enough, could not swim far enough, could not stay up late enough..."

She described herself as "...energetic...happy... bubbly [and] a friend to everyone." However, things soon changed for Lori. She mentioned a sense of doom "...settled around [her]." The camp that she once defined as beautiful became a thing of disgust, "...a thing of evil..." So began her tragic journey on the hard and often satanic and precarious road to mental health recovery. Lori stated that during one of her episodes, she did not sleep, stayed in her room and declined to go to class. She was engulfed in "...the blackness of [her] depression." Lori's father, Marvin Schiller, refused to accept the fact that she was gravely ill. Something very common in the afflicted persons themselves and their families as well. The issue of stigma is of course one of the major motivators in this scenario. Lori's dad wrote, "I didn't want my daughter to be stigmatized by some temporary rash act." Mr. Shiller thought that it was his fault that Lori was sick.

He wrote that when he was studying psychology back in the 1950's, the cause of mental illness was determined to be "...a faulty upbringing." Of course, as he stated, there were other theories. For example, the Freudian model which focused on the intrapersonal (within oneself) ideologies that the id, ego and superego were the root causes of everything. Carl Jung's concepts of unconscious myths were also considered, but most of the population believed that "...early life experiences...were behind mental disorders" Marvin Schiller wrote. Today most of us know the root causes of mental illness operates under a more holistic framework in that it has both a biological (nature) and environmental (nurture) origins. As Lori strived to survive her illness, some of her actions made it painfully obvious that she had a defiant need to transcend her "voices" or demons that threatened her very being. She struggles to grab some remnants of sanity in the midst of the insanity of her ailment. She felt that she was only a shadow of who she once was and thought that she would never return to a normal life again. However, she was determined to keep trying. Resiliency is one of the core coping strategies people often use during intense periods of trauma and strife.

Lori has hoped for something more than just being given a raw deal in the diagnosis of a disease. She foresaw a future decorated with options and opportunities. The following theories directly coincide with these innate needs and desires in the social context. Unlike Freud, who focuses on the "intrapersonal" or "within oneself" concepts, Alfred Adler, Carl Jung and Carl Rogers all offer the more practical, I think, approach in looking at the individual in relation to a more "holistic" context of their lives, particularly Jung and Adler's ideology involving *spirituality* which I will refer to later. Adler proposes a "holistic wholeness" ideology. One of the major life tasks he purports is finding where one fits in society, which includes vocation, contribution and *spirituality*. Jung proposes a similar concept of "individuation". He describes it as "...developing wholeness through integrating all the various parts of the psyche. However, Yung "...ignored the negative, maladaptive side of human nature." Nonetheless, in modern times, an increased interest in "human consciousness and human potential" has catapulted a resurrection of curiosity in Jung's ideas.

Carl Rogers also makes a similar point in that he sees the individual as heading in the path of "...wholeness, integration, [essentially] and a unified life." He believes that consciousness is engaging in the broader "...creative, formative tendency." By this he means a "directional" or "actualizing tendency", a tendency on the way to achievement, on the way to actualization that entails not only the preservation but also the improvement of the individual.

Lori made many repeated unsuccessful attempts to find and keep employment in her community. She persevered until she was able to stabilize and made small steps to getting back to the work force and feeling like a contributing member of her community and essentially her world. She found some solace in the use of prayer. Both Jung and Adler promote the idea of "spirituality" as a way to mental health recovery, and I completely agree. I know that the power of prayer, patience and perseverance have helped many on the path of recovery from mental illness.

Existentialist ideations dictate "life is meaningless or meaningful as one experiences it."

Furthermore, it defines "…regret in existentialist terms, is grief and loss over a life not lived. The best way to deal with …regret is to discover what is worth dying for is that is worth living for." So by Lori risking her life to try the then new drug Clozapine, she decided to risk dying so that she could live a fruitful life. She found meaning in suffering in that it has broadened her perspectives and enhanced her as a human being. For some, 90% of recovery can be attributed to the integration of spirituality (i.e. activities in their communities) and 10% medicinal (drug therapy). In the "Quiet Room", Lori Shiller wrote that her successful recovery process was due to the love and support that she received from family, friends and her general community; which have essentially put her on the track back from mental hell to mental health.

# The Only Way to See the Stars...

I often wonder why I smile even when sad
Thudding of my heart hearkening back
To recidivist scars running my fingers
Over the scabs abrading the cut of the
Blade and making my way in a world full
Of hurt people who hurt people
A pejorative and abortive choice
So smiling instead of snarling helps me
Remember even if bliss turns to distress
To see the stars is through the darkness

"All advocacy is, at its core, an exercise in empathy."
--Samantha Power

# PART VI
## *Advocacy*

"I'm convinced of this: Good done anywhere is good done everywhere. For a change, start by speaking to people rather than walking by them like they're stones that don't matter. As long as you're breathing, it's never too late to do some good."

Maya Angelou

# Speak up: Only You Have the Last Say in Your Mental Health Treatment Plan

*A Resilient Stance against the Mental Health Infrastructure*

Sometimes I'm not sure what I feel, if I feel or how I feel; then again sometimes I know exactly what I feel, that I feel and how I feel.

You see, I have been deemed somewhat damaged by experts who study the brain. I have been told that my brain does not function the way some normal person's should — "normal" being the questionable word here, since its true definition is up for discussion.

Hence, I have been adorned with the crown of psychopathological stigma under the vast umbrella of DSM5 or *Diagnostic and Statistical Manual 5th Edition*. The treatment for that has been to prescribe, prescribe and prescribe some more psychotropic drugs to mitigate my symptoms, thus making it possible for me to live a quasi-normal life.

But that treatment did not pan out, since consuming these innumerable experimental drugs caused me poisoning, weight imbalances and a near diabetes diagnosis. Not to mention my gradual inability to feel anything, including feeling alive!

I found myself meandering around in a daze; some said I seemed drunk when I walked, even though I have never partaken in drunken bacchanals. Eventually, experts of the phrenic nerve determined that

MAOIs, or monoamine oxidase inhibitors, among others, were only minimally helping me. They were mostly hindering me, causing my body's homeostasis to become positively unstable, just making me feel generally sick.

The experts then determined that I would benefit more from behavior modification than medicinal overconsumption. Such behavior modification modalities include Cognitive Behavior Therapy (CBT) and Dialectical Behavior therapy (DBT). Both methods of behavior therapies, although at times seemingly tiresome and boring, had positive effects on me learning to manage my symptoms, helping me learn to be proactive rather than reactive to daily life happenings.

Hence, I began the process of being weaned off the drugs for good! During the drug weaning process, I went through visceral, chemical feedback that I was not informed about nor prepared for. Apparently, after years of being on these potentially punitive prescription drugs, my mind and body grew accustomed, or dare I say "addicted" to them, the latter being a more blatant and unmitigated way of saying it.

During that period of easing off the drugs, I experienced what seemed like near death panic attacks, which were a confluence of eyes bulging, forehead sweating and sudden bursts of tachycardia or rapid heart rate. When I expressed this to my phrenic expert, he didn't seem concerned or ask me how I was doing. He simply went on with the weaning process, without outlining the process fully to me or what I could expect during it.

Looking back, I rightfully feel aggrieved by it all, but I supposed my expert did the best he could with what he knew at the time. Years later, after having some success with behavior modification therapy, my expert suggested getting back on some new drug that the pharmaceutical companies were pushing at the time.

To this I definitively replied, "Absolutely NOT!", which left him flabbergasted as he blurted out, "You've changed!"

I took that to mean he thought I was keener of mind and had found my voice since weaning off the drugs, which had also weaned me of my sense of personal power, something that people afflicted with mental illness often feel deprived of. In the words of Pulitzer Prize winning author Alice Walker of *The Color Purple* fame: "The only way you give up your power is by thinking you don't have any."

Hence, I reclaimed my personal power when I was able to feel again. I reclaimed my power when I was able to think again.

As a trained and certified human service associate, I've come to learn that sometimes vulnerable populations like those who receive mental health services aren't aware of or understand the mental health infrastructure, and more specifically, the physician reimbursement system that often dictates which drugs are being pushed their way; that the pharmaceutical companies often send seductive representatives armed with perks to help nudge them in the direction of prescribing certain drugs over others. This I learned when I had a guest speaker from the Department of Health and Human Services during one of my classes when I was achieving my Family Development certification from Tufts University.

My journey navigating psychopathology has never been linear. It has been a long, winding, arduous, destructive, constructive, prolific, stagnating, melancholy, jubilant, uncertain, hopeful path to recovery that I still partake in on a daily basis. Some days, I feel that my efforts are fatuous at best, and other days I feel unabashedly celebratory about my personal achievements on the path to mental wellness.

I have learned that if the belief that drugs are the way to well-being is not working for you, it's okay to say it's not working for you. Perhaps you need a combination of both drugs and behavior modification or perhaps not; it should be whatever works for you.

I know that drugs did not work for me. The experts themselves sometimes admit that they are experimenting with your psychological health, that they don't always know what works and what doesn't until they prescribe a new drug and wait to see what happens. Therefore, it's okay to say you're not okay with the treatment coming your way.

Remember you and only you have the last say in how you are treated. Become a spokesperson for yourself, advocate for yourself, educate yourself on treatment options, explore professional opinions, but remember the final decision rests with you.

Mental health recovery can be a stormy journey. It can and will rock your boat on unpredictable waves of highs and lows, but be not afraid on your journey. Have a map, have a plan, have an understanding of what works for you. Know where you've been, where you are and where you hope to be. In the words of literary figure Louisa May Alcott of *Little Women* fame: "I am not afraid of storms, for I am learning how to sail my ship."

I am impelled, not to squeak like a grateful and apologetic mouse, but to roar like a lion out of pride in my profession.
--John Steinbeck

# PART VII
## *Activism*

# *Roar*

against cobalt blue and black sky
hill–top silhouettes draw an undulant line
in a serpentine jungle teeming with life
amidst the deepest darkest night
moon light hovers to pet the fright
mysterious eyes carved obsidian flutter in the dusk
bottom feeders with nothing to gain groveling in the dust
furtive footsteps creeping
cranky crickets chirping
subversive sounds caballing
darkness marauding those distressing
all this and more are coalescing
but a lion's

## *ROAR*!!!
Whose colors are the colors of the morning sun and the evening sky
From pale orange to deepest flame
Induce them all to silence…

# The Ghost Dance of Echo and Shadow

The poet Carl Sandburg of *Smoke and Steel* said
"Poetry is an echo asking a shadow to dance."
So although I'm late to the party,
Mr. Shadow, will you dance with me?
For you see, I am but an Echo of my former self;

I used to have a voice before my voice lost its **roar** to *just* an echo.
Now that I'm without ego,
No longer can I boast about being or becoming a hero.
I saw your shadow silhouetted against the mountains of Montenegro,
And yearning to sound metrical
And only as an echo can ask a shadow,
Can I have this jaunty dance of the lyrical?
Together we can take a stance and reverberate in the distance,
We can prance to the rhythmic sounds of our stanzas
Dance and dance with the brazen bravery of
      Benevolence
        While eyeing delinquency,
        Teeming with culpability and
    Malevolence,
Askance…

# Random Musings about Submission

Let's just begin in
            medias res…or in the middle of things…
You see, we had artistic differences,
I was the artist and they were indifferent…
"Thank you for your submission…" but I *never*
Submitted!
At least not in the way that they *wanted* me to;
If I wasn't fiscally challenged, I would board a jet plane
And head for a luge run at Saint Moritz Switzerland,
            A psychotically dangerous sport;
Maybe they've driven me to psychosis!
Luge, a sport rooted in Germanic tribal wars against the Romans;
Bored aristocrats on vacation looking for a distraction;
Although I *am* distracted by my *own* tribal war here in America,
I am *nothing* like a bored and puerile aristocrat…
This landed me in a mawkish quagmire of
Self-pity;
In my mind I absconded into a journey of devilment to topple my
torment;
Writing can be an exercise in discernment that you are inevitably
Obliged to submit for judgment; that is if you expect to make
An impact other than justifying your own derangement due to
Maladjustment…
"Your writing is not a good fit for our publication" was the nadir of
my existence!!!
What did I write to warrant such specious offerings you may ask?
Well I wrote from the voice of an ignoble omnivorous muskrat
Whose sexual identify is non-binary;
Both a strumpet and a sthumpet!
And as an exponent of socio-political justice wrote hither and thither
An apocalyptic reverie about mutant muskrats;
A germane allegory or political fodder for the purpose of unveiling
pejorative prejudice;

Deciding to introduce a foreign element into an established
Yet *insecure* environment so to demonstrate the ensuing behavior
Of those who deem themselves superior;
The muskrat representing the only POC or person of color
In an all-white order where WASPS Rule!
WASPS being descendants of
Wealthy Anglo-Saxon Protestant Males
Feeling their long history of imposing their cultural values and
Socio-political power over *"the other"* that is
                              women and minorities...
Threatened by a neo-progressive era geared towards changing the
status quo;
Clamping down on their suppression in retaliation to the
Nascent and unrelenting movement towards socio-political
And economic progression and equality
In this American Nation!
"Thank you for your submission
But your work is not a
Good fit for our publication..." Really?!
So here I am, randomly musing about not being chosen...
Am I just a titular poet?
A deuteragonist in my own story?
When do *I* get to be the protagonist *hero despite* my **AFRO**?!
When do I get to be the plucky character in epics akin to
19th century iconoclastic South African king Shaka Zulu whose heroic
story depicted
How he united tribal factions to create notable states and powerful
African identities...or even
Anglo-Saxon and French epics like Beowulf together with Le Chanson
De Roland?
Or even the archetypal Mesopotamian great:
The Epic of Gilgamesh;
Regarded as the earliest prototypical literature and the second oldest
religious text...
"Your submission is not on par with our vision..."
Really?!

Even in the midst of global
Dissention and division?!
So we had artistic differences...I was the artist and they were indifferent.
But I decided to muse about it to manufacture
My own *moment*,
Fashion my *own* non-contentious and all-inclusive literary faction,
Where ALL postulatory voices are worthy of publication;
Because the acrimony of exclusivity is
A damnation!
I will continue to submit but NEVER to their behest for
**Submission**!!!

# Possible Causes and Effects of Cited High Blood Pressure

If your Father died of heart disease
If you have Sleep Apnea
If you have irregular sleeping schedule
If you are overweight
If you have a late night binge eating habit
If you take caffeinated Energy Supplements
If you Drink Caffeinated Tea and Hot Chocolate
If you Use heavily salted spices like Chicken Bouillon Cubes
If you're not getting enough "regular" cardio exercise
If you're inconsistent with your daily meditation practice
If you ruminate about the past: its afflictions and perceived malfeasances
If you harbor resentments regarding sociopolitical and racial injustices
If you feel constant stings of Minority Stress through Micro Aggressions of racism

If you are **BLACK**!

# Musings on the Flowering Spring of Everyday Souls

"Peace cannot be kept by force; it can only be achieved by understanding.|
Albert Einstein

Perhaps some vexed fire breathing mythical furor will immolate the
    anthropomorphic earth
Already smarting from desecration and disparagement from fellow
    anthropoids,
In a cataclysmic Inferno although already in attrition in exchange for
change,
In exchange for contrition for what and who we've wounded,
A temporary impedimenta involving pondering our own failures to
evolve
Beyond things that are tinged with an altered hue from our own…
A phalanx of obstinate, bellicose, secular, egalitarian democratic misfits
flock
    the streets in gripe
Bellies full of Teutonic pragmatism & visceral dictums of right and
wrong;
Adopting pioneering separatist ideologies of dissent against imperialists
Akin to The Great Pilgrimage to the Americas, a leitmotif of displacement and
    resilience
Throughout human history; proselytizing the proletariat to join their
cause
    with an odious sneer!
But who am I? Perhaps a perennial philosopher:
"Cogito ergo sum" or "I think therefore I am"
Thank you Rene Descartes for your rarefied ideologies…
I am an evolving being willing to listen to others involving
In the daily duties of being human, what choice does one have? But
there's
    always a "choice",
We can "choose" to evolve or we can simply dissolve by default…

I am grateful to be here on earth, grateful for the power of "choice"
Even as the world around me is seemingly crumbling...dissolving...
For over the years I have come to know that:
"Everything in [our lives] is happening to teach [us] more about
[ourselves] so even in a crisis be grateful...live in a space of gratitude..."
Thank you Oprah Winfrey for your proletarian approach to philosophy!
We are in a crisis of polarity that is deflowering our gardens
Pitting brother against brother, sister against sister, wives against husbands,
Dispute ideas and beliefs don't invalidate & dismiss the people who
have them,
don't give up on each other, all deserve to be heard and understood;
Yet we still have to remember even as we hurt, we don't have to suffer,
However!
"Out of suffering have emerged the strongest souls; the most massive
characters are seared with scars." Thank you Khalil Gibran for your tarry
        pansophy.
Open your heart to your scars, befriend your scars, let wounds of
The past strengthen and heal you rather than weaken & hurt you;
Even as we get angry, we don't have to forfeit our ability to be joyful,
It is not happiness that makes us grateful, it is gratefulness that makes
us happy...
We can find our strength in our weakness, for "God's strength is made
perfect in weakness" Thank you Corinthians: 2. Keeping in mind that
the early mystics
        perceived
God without subjecting him to tangible proof...
Name calling is the last refuge of the monosyllabic;
Be mindful of your words and resist engaging in
Gratuitous verbal violence of the morally virulent and their unasinous ilk
Amidst the clamor of contrived and nebulous directives for divisions;
Know that what's meant for you will never miss you and
What misses you was never meant for you,

Anything that has your attention becomes your energy and manifests itself into your existence, Evoke Emanuel Kant's first rule in his categorical imperative
 philosophy:
"Don't use other human beings as a means to an end"
Remember! we are products of our past not prisoners of it...
May the best of your yesterday be the worst of your *tomorrow!*

# The Way You Give Up Power:
## An Ode to the Oppressed

"When power leads man toward arrogance, poetry remind him of his limitations. When power narrows the area of man's concern, poetry remind him of the richness and diversity of existence. When power corrupts, poetry cleanses."

John F. Kennedy

Hey you, Mr. Power!
Why should I shrink so that you should thrive?!
Why are you telling me who I am?!
Why are you telling me what I am?!
Why should you live in a palace while I live in a dive?!
Why are you telling me how I can or cannot?!
Don't you know I know who I am?
I am a descendant of the first civilization on this planet…
The Africans who were so that you are…
My voice is sacrosanct!
The Africans who could so that you would later colonize and caponize their dignity!
Your historic proclivity to gravitate towards power doesn't
Necessitate me to facilitate your SUPREME cause to suppress
You have caused enough distress!
Now it's time for progress and as a progressive
I don't give you the power to overpower ME!
In the words of African descendant Alice Walker:
"The only way you give up your power
Is by thinking you don't have any."
Gradually, my power is finally seeking its sortie
Hey, Mr. Power?
Why should I
*Shrink*
*So that you should*

**thrive**?!

# Waiting for Justification

"All truth passes through three stages. First, it is ridiculed. Second, it is
violently opposed. Third, it is accepted as being self-evident."

Arthur Schopenhauer

Stranded in desolate "mako cica" or Badlands,
I look around my environs
To find myself feeling full of fear and
Empty,
Wistfully wishing for
Fearless freedom replete with bravery and
Climactic ascendency from soul
poverty;
For you see, twenty-twenty was a bad year for me…
But me and you represent WE and so was it for you too?
"We" had to face a faceless pandemic
Known as the Coronavirus;
"Corona" actually means "Crown";
Corona…a crowning achievement and failure of humanity?
Exposed the inequities of society;
Then of course there was George Floyd!
Another Black man who had to die to change the world;
Rid it of its unjustified ways when it comes to
Capricious acts of the unjust against those who don't look the same way;
That is the "White" way…cause if you're not White, then you must
be Wrong!
As you may recall before George Floyd, there was another Black man
in 1994,
The plaintive call of Rodney King who after a
Vicious beating by Los Angeles police also caught on video cried
*"WHY CAN'T WE ALL JUST GET ALONG?!"*
George Floy's turn was a long time coming and came it did;
When he too cried out
*"I CAN'T BREATHE!!!"*

Now is that "just" if we are to all "get along"?

That day, history's race story was broadcasted LIVE for all to see;

America had long denied its pandemic poison known as racism;

Citizens treated like denizens from a demimonde was the

Crowning achievement of the Coronavirus;

Exposing the virulence of racial intolerance and malfeasance;

But it also brought the world together, albeit in horror to stand
*TOGETHER!*

Had it not been for the confiscating power of Corona,

Americans would not have been home in the suburbs and urbania,

To watch the just begging from *under the knee* of the unjust to "Breathe"
drama in the media!

We were all on the fringes that day,

All who were deemed "*different*"

Waiting hoping for justice to unjustify the

Traumatization of *THE OTHER* under American weather...

"WE CAN'T BREATHE" is our collective cry for the just to *step-UP*!

Because your silence equals consent equals violence!

Centuries of killings of Blacks for being Black MUST STOP!

Stop the criminalization of a color in a child's Crayola box;

So then Corona came and *stepped-up* that day!

A virus that doesn't discriminate and put *HATE* on display, exposing
it for all to see on the TV;

I stand stranded in the middle of nowhere, suffocating on dogged dusts
seizing my throat

"*I can barely breathe...*"

Like an endangered species, a mockingbird to kill without witnesses,

Like a stereotyped target in the desert of condemnation,

And as amelioration of my situation came a

Cop car with two cops from the cop station,

The Officers offered me a ride to the courthouse;

Where I HOPE and pray for *justification*...

Happiness can exist only in acceptance.
--George Orwell

# PART VIII

## *Acceptance*

*"Do the best you can until you know better, then when you know better, do better."* — Maya Angelou

## Exploring Self-Love in "You Are Enough: The Journey to Accepting Your Authentic Self"

Who among us have not heard that inner voice gaslighting us by reinforcing the mantra "You are not good enough"? Humans are plagued with incessant feelings of uncertainty about who we are. We live in a society that constantly ingrains in our consciousness — and to a more pernicious extent, subconscious — that we are somehow inadequate while navigating life on this planet.

One of the components contributing to this enigma of the nature of the psyche is that we constantly compare ourselves to others. We think we should be who we think others are. We think we should have what others have. However, by participating in this type of rumination we deprive ourselves of what we could actually be if we focused on our own set of talents and Earthly gifts. What was meant for you does not necessarily align with my <u>authentic</u> self and vice versa.

I find myself coming alive when I focus on the things that bring me joy, the things I am passionate about and the things that I look forward to doing. Whether that be writing, exercising, reading a good book or the pleasure I get from watching my favorite episode of reality TV, what makes me smile may not be what makes you smile. That has to be okay if we are to find our own joys while navigating our own paths.

Comparing ourselves to others can compress our possibilities for potential <u>growth</u> in all areas of our lives. When you're on the right path, things just magically seem to fall into place. You do not have to try to manipulate the environment around you to get desired results. In the words of Pulitzer Prize winning author Alice Walker of *The Color Purple* fame, "The right path disappears beneath your feet."

Suffering in life only comes when you resist the natural flow of things, thus the wisdom in "going with the flow." In the words of the late spiritual guru Ram Dass, "Resistance to the unpleasant situation is the root of suffering." Essentially, we must embrace our defeats just as we rejoice over our victories. We must follow the energy that awakens the fire of the heart, and greet life with gusto and optimism, not sorrow and pessimism. Do not allow misconceived notions of who you think you're supposed to be, keep you from being who you were meant to be.

## Finding Your Own Way

When you've skidded off your path in life, you'll find that your pathological ruminations run amok. Every step you take becomes more and more frazzled with uncertainty, which ignites massive insecurities and demoralizing self-doubt. It can be helpful to counter this psychological attack with a technique called opposite action used in cognitive behavior therapy.

Opposite action means negating what your mind is telling you is true. If it's telling you that you are a loser, then you counteract that with, "Well, although I've suffered losses, I've also achieved many gains," and then list them. Opposite action allows you to recalibrate your path and trajectory, despite the push back from your pathological mind that is preprogramed with past hurts and failures.

While all humans have a natural aversion to pain and we don't like to be uncomfortable, discomfort can pave the way forward along our healing paths. It is said that, "A comfort zone is a beautiful place, but nothing ever grows there." Growth requires stretching into zones of discomfort and the uncertainty of what is unfamiliar. In his podcast *Doing the Real Work to Free yourself*, author Michael Singer asserts that, "Sometimes the deepest pain is what pushes you to your highest self…. It is in the moments of freefall that you find your wings." Instead of "[finding their] wings", our society is increasingly involved with the practice of conspicuous consumption; designer labels and the latest technology take precedence—over soul searching and discovering their sense of personal authenticity—and is of particular importance in the ostentatious display of theatrical materialism. Rather than being concerned with showing how much money you have or making more money, why not adapt a new personal paradigm by making more of yourself?

## Dr. Wayne Dyer's 5 Lessons to Live By

In closing I would like to share the late Dr. Wayne Dyer's "5 Lessons to Live By" that will help anyone trekking their own path to personal awakening.

1. When you change the way you look at things, the things you look at change.
2. There are no justified resentments.
3. What you think is what you become.
4. Be open to everything and attached to nothing.
5. Don't die with music still in you.

# The Dimming of a Summer's Day

Ugh!
A Sudden winter shower has chilled
Shuddered and shrouded the summer air
This shift of the sun isn't rare
Just the dawning of the awakening of some other reality.
Whatever happened to the jollity
Enjoyed similarly just seasons before?
Before Mr. Winter took away the summer's gold!
Mr. Frost was cold
But was right to say
Nothing gold can **EVER** stay

Just like *the dimming of a Summer's day...*

"In the absence of Light, look closer and you will see a spark!"

--Jacques Fleury

## *About the Author*

**J**acques **Stanley Fleury** is a Haitian-American Poet, Educator and author of four books thus far. He holds an undergraduate degree in Liberal Arts and is currently pursuing graduate studies in the fine arts at Harvard University online. Once on the editing staff of The Watermark, a literary magazine at the University of Massachusetts, his first book Sparks in the Dark: A Lighter Shade of Blue, A Poetic Memoir was featured in and endorsed by the Boston Globe. His second book: It's Always Sunrise Somewhere and Other Stories is a collection of short fictional stories dealing with the human condition as the characters navigate life's foibles and was featured on Good Reads. His current book and hitherto magnum opus Chain Letter to America: The One Thing You Can Do to End Racism, A Collection of Essays, Fiction and Poetry Celebrating Multiculturalism is available at The Harvard Book Store, Barnes and Noble and Amazon. His work has been published by Poets Reading The News, Oddball Magazine, The Boston Haitian Reporter, the Haitian trilingual journal of political and literary studies TANBOU, Spare Change News, The Somerville Times, Patch News, Boston Events Insider, The International Network of Street Newspapers (INSP) reaching over 120 countries and languages, 'HOME Anthology' of prose and poetry edited by Anne Brudevold of Eden Waters Press, the Cornell University Press anthology 'Class Lives: Stories from across Our Economic Divide' edited by Chuck Collins et al, Muddy River Poetry Review among local and worldwide Poet Laureates and the international Cooch Behar Anthology series of poetry edited by Sourav Sarkar, Litterateur Redefining World Magazine edited by Anthru Shajil, both world renown poets & literary figures based out of India. He was the Official Poet for the Annual Urban Walk for Haiti and has made personal appearances at many Boston and Cambridge area venues including Harvard and North Eastern Universities and many others. His Cd A Lighter Shade of Blue as a lyrics writer in collaboration with the neo-folk musical group Sweet Wednesday is available on Amazon, iTunes & Spotify to benefit Haitian charity St. Boniface. He is Cantabrigian living in the great state of Massachusetts.

# *Influences*

Some of my major influences have been my English teachers at Boston English High School who introduced me to William Shakespeare of Stratford-upon-Avon, England of the English Renaissance Theater Genre. After studying Julius Caesar, I was inspired by the orbiting electrons by the waters of the muses to write my first poem about civil rights iconoclast and national historical figure Dr. Martin Luther King Jr., ; which ended up being published in the school literary magazine EXPRESSIONS.

My influences continued throughout my college years and even post college when I immersed myself with writers, authors, professors, and journalists, all of whom propelled my writing on a path to lapidary clarity and precision through discipline and craftsmanship. To them I am forever indebted...

www.facebook.com/J.S.Fleury.

## Birth Place

port--au-prince, Haiti
Nationality: American

## Accomplishments

Author of (4) Books of Essays, Fiction and Poetry and Featured in (8) anthologies

Two books Archived in the permanent research special collections section at the University of Massachusetts Boston's Healey Library
National Dean's List Honoree

Former Television Host/Producer of "Dream Weavers" at Cambridge Community Television (CCTV)

Official Poet for the Annual Urban Walk for Haiti

Lyrics Writer for folk musical group Sweet Wednesday

Certified Tutor (College of Learning & Reading Association)

Provider of Human Services Certificate

Top Three Finalist for Valedictorian in College

National College Honor Society Inductee
Member of the Phi Theta Kappa International Honor Society

Student Government Recognition Award

Computer Programming/Business Communications Diploma
Who's Who Among America's High School Students

Member of the Business Professionals of America

Son, Brother, Uncle, Friend & Community volunteer

## Additional Information

I have published Poetry, articles, essays about the history of Haiti, African-American & United States History, the Civil War, Oppressive Pedagogy, Fiction, original Haitian Folklore, critical reviews of English, Russian, Irish and American literature, theater reviews etc... In addition to my professional pursuits, some of my more personal ventures include a regular practice of Yoga, Pilates and Meditation to connect with my visceral and ethereal self and have come to understand that the truth of who we are is not "I am this" or "I am that" but "I am." I, like Herman Hesse, truly believe that "the true profession of man is finding his way to himself"...

Printed in the United States
by Baker & Taylor Publisher Services